Here Today, Hired Tomorrow
A PRACTICAL GUIDE TO GETTING THE JOB YOU WANT FAST

KURT KIRTON

Facebook - www.facebook.com/authorkk

LinkedIn - www.linkedin.com/in/kurtkirton

Newsletter - Subscribe at www.bit.ly/kwknewsltr

Twitter - www.twitter.com/kurtkirton

Website/Blog - www.kurtkirton.com

YOOPER
PUBLICATIONS
BUSINESS

P.O. Box 158262
Nashville, TN 37215
www.yooperpublications.com

Here Today, Hired Tomorrow
© MMXV Yooper Publications

ISBN-13: 978-1-941558-06-5
ISBN-10: 1941558062

Library of Congress Control Number: 2015932612
Printed in the United States of America

Warning and Disclaimer

Bio: Jennifer Nash (http://about.me/jennifer.nash)
Consultation: Ephiphany Creative Services (www.your-epiphany.com)
Editor: Ellen Margulies (www.linkedin.com/in/ellenmargulies)
Cover: Graeme Morris, Wam/Bam/Creative (www.wambamcreative.com)
Graphic Design and Layout: Kurt Kirton
Proofreaders: Jennifer Nash and Betsy Koch (http://bit.ly/ewkoch)

CONTENTS AT A GLANCE

Table of Contents

INTRODUCTION

So you may be wondering who I am and why I'm an expert on job searching and giving you advice on yours. Well, here's my story. My background has spanned everything from advertising, marketing, and the printing industry to office management and call center work. I've been laid off 6—count 'em—6 times in my career! I'd love to be able to say that my work experience over the past 15 years has all been research in order to write this book—something like J. A. Jacobs (author of *The Year of Living Biblically* and *Know-It-All*) would do. But that's not the case. Allow me to explain.

After living in Nashville, Tennessee for a few years, I finally achieved one of my dreams and landed a position on the business side of the music industry. Sadly, Napster birthed about the same time and shook up the music world big time. What followed were 4 layoffs.

At 3 of the 4 music companies, I worked for the same supervisor (a great and competent leader whom I respect). So I looked forward to continuing that work relationship, hoping that each successive position would last, perpetuating my dream. Unfortunately, these record labels and music dot coms either closed or cut staff. And the others? The layoffs I experienced after my music industry days were due to downsizing, restructuring, etc. Then, of course, I'd had my fair share of those few jobs I had to leave—be they stop-gap, relocation-related, or just a downright bad fit—all adding up to more job searches than I'd wish on my worst enemy!

WHY THIS BOOK?

I've now been through the job search process so often that I've developed a proven system. No one I've ever met *loves* looking for a new job, and without the structure of a system to work within, you'll end up feeling like you're floundering, overwhelmed, or scattered.

In this book, I want to share my system along with other insights—some of them traditional and some from the latest schools of thought. This book draws upon knowledge and resources from colleagues, headhunters, HR/Department of Labor professionals, outplacement services, and other experts. Moreover, it includes practical templates, scripts, lists, and samples to help you cut to the chase and get productive in your search quickly. My mission is to shorten the time you're in transition and help you get back to work—ideally in a job you enjoy that's in your field of interest.

Another reason I wrote this book is because there's such an incredible amount of resources at your disposal, and you're likely to receive so much advice and differing opinions from everyone in your life that it can be overwhelming. Where do you start? How do you better deal with the feelings of being laid off? How do you make the best use of your time? How do you organize all the information you'll run across? How can you expedite your path to the right job? This book will answer these questions.

And just FYI, while in the midst of writing this book, twice I landed the jobs I wanted on my terms (once in about 6 months, and once in 5) by following the techniques and using the resources I'll teach you. This could be you; read on!

THE STATE OF THE WORLD

Job security? Unfortunately, I don't think many occupations include this anymore! This quote from a company review posted at www.glassdoor.com by a former employee is so on point nowadays: "Employees are not treated with respect; they are expendable." It's a sad thing, but for most of us, it's the world we live in now. Companies treat employees more and more like they're expendable, despite their dedication, hard work, accomplishments, and even hanging in through rough times with their raises on hold.

And getting hired is no longer a once-in-a-lifetime experience where you work for the same company until you retire. People face 6 to 10 or more job changes during their working life, on average. Further, the economy and globalization both affect the job market. Changing jobs and being in career transition more frequently is a reality for almost everyone now—more than any other time I can recall in my lifetime.

There are some positive outcomes from all of this. It's leveling out the playing field—in other words, people like me who may have felt like pariahs because they have several layoffs in their work history now know they're not alone. And employers are fine with seeing 3+ years at each position on a résumé since they're happy to get a minimum of 3 years out of you. But with so many people (including the never ending tide of college graduates) on the hunt, you still need a leg up—something to give you an edge in your search.

NO MAGIC BULLET

Despite the title of this book, I can't define what "fast" is for you. I'm not going to tell you that just because you follow my advice to a "T" that you'll have your dream job in 48 days, 4 months, etc. Here's why: A friend of mine was laid off from his scientific research position at a local university. His job search took about a year and a half, since most companies in town did not have the type of position he wanted. So his target market was the entire US—quite a challenge. Eventually, he started writing online articles on topics in his field at a scientific website to help boost his visibility during his job search. Finally, after much effort and tenacity, he landed a great position at Yale.

Obviously, everyone would love to have a job search that only lasted a few days or weeks—another friend of mine switched jobs almost seamlessly between 2 companies, twice! But how long your search takes will depend on several factors: your field and whether you're changing fields, your level of expertise/experience, your diligence at the job search, your ability to network and present yourself, and whether you're seeking something out of your current state or country.

SCOPE

The scope of this book will not include searching for a job out of state or country, but I can offer a few tips that will help. If you're financially able to do so, go ahead and move to your city of choice. That's what I did with my move from Mississippi to Nashville. Frequently, employers are skeptical that out-of-state applicants will actually move if they get the position, so they're hesitant to invest the time to interview and consider them. Or they don't want to be expected to pay for relocation expenses. Second, network at associations, churches, and activity groups (like www.meetup.com groups) in your new city, and put the word out to your social network ahead of time that you're moving. And of course, you can do what my friend did and write pieces for websites with subject material in your field to get your name out there.

If you are thinking about moving but are not sure where, www.findyourspot.com has a great quiz that can make location recommendations based on your answers. If you do have an idea where you'd like to go, try www.bestplaces.net. There, you can research by city.

Finally, if you're currently employed but searching for a new job, you can use the same systems I'll cover in the book. Your search will just be more challenging since you'll have less free time than someone who's unemployed. But lunch hours, before and after work, and weekends are great times to further your search.

Think about it like doing a pared-down version of my system. And of course, depending on your situation, stay stealthy with your interviewing efforts and LinkedIn profile (verbiage and preferences) to avoid rocking the boat at your current company. I, too, have done the "look for another job while being employed full-time" method, and it was just as tough as not working and looking for my next position. So, hats off to you if this is your situation.

Whatever scenario you're facing with your job search, feel good that you're holding one of the major solutions in your hand—this book. Try following this system, and adapt it to best suit you. Let's get started!

NOTE: Access *www.kurtkirton.com/hthtfiles.zip* to download a zip file of most of the forms and templates mentioned in the book or shown in the Appendix. This way you can easily modify them for your use without having to spend your valuable time recreating them.

I've Fallen but I Can Get Up
Chapter for the Unemployed

If you've lost your job, I am truly sorry. If you've read the Introduction, you know that if anyone can understand what you're going through, it's me.

During one of my periods of transition, my pastor said something that got my attention: "None of us want to change, even if it's for the good. Until you're cut to the heart, you'll rarely make a significant change. Sacrificial actions are needed to make authentic change." Career transition is definitely a challenge that cuts to the heart and requires sacrifice and discipline. You sometimes hear the old adage, "Everything happens for a reason." I don't think anyone initially likes to hear that or think that way after something as traumatic as a layoff or firing, but you tend to gain a little perspective after time passes and the shock wears off.

My last couple of job losses were definitely a plus. They allowed me time to seek help for chronic tension headaches, finish contracting the detached garage I had built, and make big strides in working on several large projects I'd previously had nothing but a bit of weekend time for.

♛ NOTE--- I am not a product of my circumstances. I am a product of my decisions.
–Stephen Covey

ADDRESS THE GREEN FIRST

Okay, let's jump in. You lost your job. What to do now? Most of what stressed me out the day of my last layoff was going from my full salary to unemployment pay. The first thing you need to do is get a good look at your financial picture by drafting a new budget. Figure out how much you'll bring in from unemployment, how much you have in savings, and factor in any severance or separation pay and other sources of income.

If at all possible, you want to avoid any taxes or early withdrawal penalties that may result from tapping into your 401k or IRA. Sit down, and start with the basics—rent/mortgage, utilities, car payment, etc. —and make a new budget based on this amount. For help with this and a sample budget, see by blog post at http://bit.ly/5btools.

If you need to take a stop-gap type job to make more money than unemployment benefits provide, do so without worry. Employers are far more likely to base the salary of your new position on what you earned at your last professional job than what you earn in a temporary situation. Later on, remember to roll the 401k's from your previous position into an IRA or another saving product.

UNEMPLOYMENT BENEFITS

If you were let go for a qualifying reason (lack of work, downsizing, etc.) and you did not quit, file for your unemployment pay benefits right away. Don't be too proud to claim this. Your employer pays into a fund for just such situations. You worked hard and deserve this benefit to help get you to your next position. And regardless of whether you also get a severance package, you are still entitled to apply for unemployment benefits, unless you signed an agreement to the contrary when you were hired.

Requirements and the nuts and bolts of unemployment will vary by state, but here's a general idea of how it will go: If your state is like Tennessee, nearly all unemployment claims must be filed online (only by phone if you have a special reason you were let go). Filing online will get your claim into the system far faster than trying for weeks to get through a phone tree and wait on hold for eons to talk to a live person!

A quick online search should yield the correct web page at which to file for unemployment benefits in your state. If not, ask a friend, or check the blue pages in your phone book, and call the Department of Labor to get instructions on how to file your claim online. Keep a document to track this process. Include the date you file, the dates you check on the status of your claim, and the names of anyone you meet or speak with. Benefits could take from 3 to 10 weeks to begin, depending on how backlogged your state's processing is and whether your case needs special review. Pay will most likely be weekly and via direct deposit.

You'll probably receive an information sheet in the mail detailing things like how and when to file weekly certifications, how much you can earn without reducing your weekly benefit or canceling your unemployment pay completely, and whether your state requires you to apply for a certain number of jobs per week. Make sure you read and understand this information, since you are legally responsible to abide by it while drawing unemployment benefits. Designate a file folder or drawer where you can keep all documentation you receive from the state.

THE IMPORTANCE OF HEALTH INSURANCE

I never recommend going without insurance. Who's to say you won't have an expensive car wreck or be diagnosed with a costly medical condition during your transition? There's no free ride for the unemployed. Here's a story to illustrate.

Once when I was a temp between jobs, about 4:00am one morning I thought I might be having a heart attack. Despite high hopes that it was simple heartburn, after checking with the 24-hour nurse line, which was a benefit of my insurance, I had to go to the emergency room. After everything turned out alright, and the bills started arriving, I was able to bargain down the amount I owed a bit with the main care provider. With insurance, my responsibility was around $1200. Without, the total would have probably been at least $4,000!

If you end up with a whopper of a total, a hospital will just put you on a payment plan—and for a very long time if it's an expensive medical situation. Although some hospitals may reduce the bill somewhat, there's no free pass just because you're unemployed. So it's wise to find a way to have at least basic health insurance. Frequently, the cost of your former employer's COBRA coverage is prohibitive. So you can also look into how the Affordable Care Act system (www.healthcare.gov) can help you.

♛ NOTE--- At the point you need prescriptions, shop around for the least expensive pharmacy. I find that Costco usually has the lowest price, and you do not have to be a member to use its pharmacy. And depending on the drug, frequently there are significant savings to be had by calling around and switching to generics for many drugs. In addition, some stores like Walgreen's offer a prescription savings membership that may save you more than it costs.

HIT THE GROUND RUNNING

As you move through this process, you may feel overwhelmed. There are just so many things you need to do to get started looking for your next position. But remember, there is time—especially if you've started your unemployment benefits, and ideally, have some savings put back. You don't just jump gung ho into your first football game of the season without having gathered the proper equipment, interacted with your teammates and coach, gotten fit, and done some training. The same holds true for your job search: You'll want to prepare and have a plan.

Don't panic. Just keep track of all the things you need to do as you think of them. Use an Action Plan to prioritize anything you think of that you need to do (see the template in chapter 3, or download the one online at *www.kurtkirton.com/hthtfiles.zip* for a quick start making your own.)

This will provide you with a sequenced work flow from which to operate; it will pay off to do things in order.

You'll want to craft your "elevator speech"—a 10- to 15-second response to the question, "So, what do you do?" We'll talk more about this in the Action Plan chapter. Just spin it positively as you begin to think about what you want to say. When networking, or even when talking with friends, always say, "I'm in transition right now" or "I'm a ___ (your profession.)" Even saying, "I'm between jobs" is better than branding yourself as "unemployed." Avoid using the "u" word.

IT'S OKAY TO CHILL OUT

At least for me, there's a tendency to feel like I shouldn't enjoy anything because (and while) I'm in transition. It's natural to want to beat yourself up or throw the occasional pity party. But there's no need for that. No matter how grim it seems at times, don't succumb to the thought that unemployment is going to be forever or that you're now blacklisted by every company in your industry.

It's important to try to enjoy life during this time. Do try to be as productive as possible each day as you conduct your job search, but allow yourself to be happy and have a social life. I really like the story by Marlane Peak (a Team Development and Training Specialist at a large book publisher here in Nashville) that I found at a regular weekly networking meeting here in the greater Nashville area. Her story "A Divine Holiday" is in the Epilogue. Take a moment to read it.

BOOTING THE CHIP

Being laid off is one of the most challenging things that can happen in life. It may make you feel disposable, shafted, slighted, angry, and depressed. After my fifth layoff, I remember the stages for me were shock, questioning, anger, and finally acceptance.

Before you even begin to look for your next position, you should do some soul-searching and ask yourself whether you're holding onto any hint of negativity, resentment, anger, etc., about your situation. If you are, you'll want to get that chip off your shoulder. HR professionals and hiring managers can frequently pick up on the fact that you are negative, bitter, or holding a grudge against your former employer. You don't want to come across like a wounded animal.

I think the emotional weight we bear as a result of a layoff is too much of a burden to put on a friend over and over. It's also embarrassing—even with your closest friends—to talk about your deepest feelings. Still, you need to be honest about these feelings in order to work through them and come out the other side stronger and ready to pound the pavement.

I recommend talking to your pastor, a psychologist, or a Stephen Minister (an unbiased confidential lay person who's trained to listen and provide care and support at no cost to those in crisis or difficult life situations). Google "Stephen Ministers" plus your city to find churches that can get you in touch with one.

It was such a support and encouragement to me to have Wynn Batson, my Stephen Minister, listen and give me advice. He was actually a supervisor and hiring manager at his company and had some great perspective. Don't be ashamed to seek out support, or apprehensive to talk to someone new about your feelings and situation. Having a shoulder to lean on and someone to listen will help you get back on your feet faster than going it alone.

The support of family, friends, and colleagues is also important during this time. But before you start to tell them, you may want to take a few days alone to get through the initial shock. It's better to be positive when you start letting those close to you know what happened. People are more likely to want to be around and help someone who's confident and positive. But definitely let them know you are available for new work. (We'll go over this in chapter 3). You'll want to have a few close friends (and some may be in transition themselves) you can lean on during your job search when you need them.

CUE THE THEME FROM *ROCKY*

Okay, so we've addressed getting your mind and attitude in shape. It's also important to stay—or get—in good physical condition. Don't allow being down or working from home on your job search (and being around the fridge more!) to put you in a bad habit of eating poorly or snacking too much. Be mindful of what you eat and how much. Develop and maintain a fitness routine.

If you can't afford a regular gym membership during this time, consider a community center or even walking around your neighborhood. Getting regular exercise, even if it's just walking for half an hour 3-4 times a week, will help stave off depression and keep your energy level up. This will come in handy as you manage yourself during your job search and help you maintain positive energy as you network and interview.

SKILL SHARPNESS

If you want to stay in your field, you'll also want to keep up your skills and knowledge. Read trade magazines or industry blogs. Occasionally attend a seminar or association webinar. Make sure you're up on the software used in your profession. Pay attention to your local news stations and publications so you can be in the know on national and local news. If you're like me and don't watch much TV, you can always catch the news on the radio (for instance, NPR) as you're driving.

♛ NOTE--- If you have a severance package, take advantage of any perks your company may have given you—things such as outplacement resources like Right Management, extended insurance, online training courses, etc.

INTERNSHIPS

Being a student fresh out of college in this day and age is more challenging than ever. I worked summers and Christmas breaks during college because I needed the money, as most students do. And I coveted my study and free time during the semesters and never did an internship. Although most are unpaid, an internship is one of the best ways to meet, work, and network with movers and shakers in your field of interest—not to mention giving hiring managers a taste of the great work you're capable of and a snapshot of your reliability, creativity, and work ethic.

At least at Belmont University here in Nashville, there are more companies wanting interns than there are students wanting internships! Go, supply and demand! So use that advantage to seek out and choose the best internship opportunity for you.

Consider doing an internship at one of your top target companies if you can afford the opportunity cost (the cost, in time, money, or other benefits, of following one course of action over another). If you need to work a paying job during college, try doing the internship the summer before your final year. Or, better yet, consider interning during your last semester. Just make sure to contact the companies you're considering in late summer to check whether a spring-only internship is an option, since some may only offer a fall-and-spring option. This way, you won't be blindsided and miss the boat on a great opportunity.

While interning, you'll get firsthand, real world knowledge, ideally in a position similar to what you'll be doing once you graduate. This could give you an advantage over applicants unknown to the company and net you a full-time job after graduation. Even if you are not hired on afterwards, a reference from your manager and the opportunities you'll have to network during the internship can be valuable tools in your efforts toward a solid first job. While networking, you could meet someone at another company that could end up hiring you down the road. At worst, you'll be able to start building your network.

RECAP:

1. Make a temporary budget.
2. File for unemployment benefits, keeping notes on this process.
3. Set up temporary health insurance.
4. Keep track of things you think of you need to do using the Action Plan.
5. Relax.
6. Talk to someone trusted to dispel any chips on your shoulder.
7. Stay active, and attend to your physical fitness.
8. Keep your skills in your line of work updated, and get any training you need.
9. If you're a student, consider an internship before you graduate.

Other Reading:

- *Don't Waste Your Sorrows: New Insight Into God's Eternal Purpose for Each Christian in the Midst of Life's Greatest Adversities* by Paul Billheimer
- *We Got Fired* by Harvey Mackay (If you feel like you were done wrong in your layoff or termination, this may prove therapeutic and help get the chip off your shoulder.)
- *Why Did I Lose My Job If God Loves Me* by Rick Pritikin

Resources For Mature Job Seekers:

- www.aarp.org
- www.go60.com/older-workers.html
- www.ncoa.org
- Check if your state government has a section of its website for job search advice.

.

2

All Systems Go
Getting Started

♛ NOTE--- Why do athletes make so much money? Because they know what their talent is and can demonstrate it on the field. So prepare like an athlete. Think of yourself as a brand, and come up with a plan for yourself just like you would for a product or service. Manage your brand thoughtfully while understanding the challenges you have and need to overcome. When crafting your personal creative strategy, consider your unique qualities and what makes you credible and authentic. And most important when branding yourself, just *be* yourself.[1]

Alright, so you are either looking for a new position, have lost your job, or are seeking your first full-time job. Resist the temptation to start flinging résumés at lots of online job postings on sites like www.careerbuilder.com, www.monster.com, etc. Like we covered in the previous chapter, you need to get your plan and supplies together before you dive in. Let's look at a few things you should do at this stage. Then, we'll get really practical in the next chapter by crafting your Action Plan!

ATTITUDE

To pass the time on the stationary bike at my gym one day, I was reading *The New Yorker*. This magazine is peppered with cartoons that don't necessarily relate to the content near them. I laughed out loud at one in particular by Barbara Smaller. A college student sitting in the career counselor's office at his university with a chipper look on his face states, "I'd like one of those careers where you make a six-figure income while wearing a T-shirt and sweatpants." The look on the counselor's face is priceless—somber, not amused, and I'm sure thinking, "Buddy, get a clue."

While just about no one starts off with their dream job, it doesn't hurt to maintain a positive state of mind as you search. Further, it will especially help you reach your high paying, T-shirt wearing, get up late every day job goal to lay some groundwork to start the process off right.

YOUR SITUATION

So, think about this… you can either:

1. Do the same role at a different company in the same industry
2. Do the same role in a different industry
3. Do a different role in the same industry or
4. Seek a different role in a whole new industry

Similarly, and depending on your current situation, you're either looking for:

1. A stop-gap or survival job—something entry level that you want to do for a certain reason or for a finite time (like working so you can take college classes, supplement your current income, or care for your new baby).
2. A job to complement your current career path, such as the same type of job but with a new company, or
3. A new career direction—changing what you're doing significantly. You'll want to seek out expertise on this option by reading books like *What Color Is Your Parachute?* by Richard Bolles or *Fearless Career Change* by Marky Stein, since this route falls outside the scope of this book.

♛ NOTE--- Changing industries can make for a challenging but do-able job search. A career coach at your local Department of Labor, outplacement service rep, or life coach can be of assistance in helping you re-invent yourself. They can also advise you on your résumé, help you craft your exit statement, give input on your elevator speech, and be an all around great resource on most things job search related. If you don't live close enough to a Department of Labor and are able to pay a fee, you can contact the National Career Development Association at www.ncda.org. All are licensed professional counselors. Rates will vary according to the services provided.

DO WHAT YOU LOVE

If you don't know what you want to do, how can anyone help you? It's important before starting a job search to decide this and make sure you're looking for something you *like* doing, not just something you've been doing or are good at. Your passion for what you like and want to do will drive what job you are seeking.

On the way out of a dental appointment one day years ago, my longtime dentist here in Nashville, Dr. Michael Thomason, announced he'd be turning over his practice to someone else. I asked him why, and he replied that he was leaving to pursue a career as an elementary school teacher. What a radical change! My immediate response was, "You must have read *48 Days To The Work*

You Love by Dan Miller." He said yes. Knowing where he was coming from, I wished him the best and told him I'd miss his dentistry (since he was one of the best.)

If you've read *48 Days…*, you know that Miller encourages readers to figure out what they're really passionate about and make *that* their career. While this concept is challenging and somewhat idealistic, it's a basic one to consider before you get very far into a job search. Legendary Apple founder Steve Jobs said it so well:

> "Your work is going to fill a large part of your life, and the only way to be truly satisfied is to do what you believe is great work. And the only way to do great work is to love what you do. If you haven't found it yet, keep looking. As with all matters of the heart, you'll know when you find it. And like any great relationship, it just gets better and better as the years roll on. So keep looking until you find it. Don't settle."

APTITUDE TOOLS

A career assessment can help give you a better understanding of yourself and clarify ideas for careers that would be a good fit for you. The Birkman First Look (a proprietary version of a larger assessment that is presented by The Birkman Method) will analyze your career orientation, management style, and job strengths. It can help you understand your level of proficiency in planning, administrating, communicating, and expediting; identify your ideal work environment; and suggest jobs you should consider based on how you score within a list of career categories.

If you do not want to pay to take something like The Birkman First Look, there are some free and low-cost tools. One is O*Net Interest Profiler (www.onetcenter.org/IP.html), and you can also check out Tom Rath's book *StrengthsFinder 2.0* and the online resource by the same name (www.strengthsfinder.com.) There are many other resources along this line at www.quintcareers.com/career_assessment.html.

Bear in mind, the free assessments are somewhat subjective and don't have the capacity to yield dead-on results with absolute precision. They should be used as a guide. You can contact your local Department of Labor to see which tests they use. Furthermore, they may cover the charge for paid assessments like The Birkman First Look, Myers Briggs, or Strong Interest Inventory and can have a career coach review and discuss the results with you.

Assessments are good ways to learn more about yourself in relationship to your career interests, but always use the results as a loose guideline, and temper them with your judgment, goals, and interests. If you decide to do one, after getting your results, make sure to also consider what activities you enjoy most, your work style, what you need from others, how you react under stress, and what job titles interest you and seem to be a good fit. Then, spin your résumé and elevator speech in support of the profession you choose, focusing on and branding yourself as a competent ___ (fill in the blank for you). Guidance and tips on elevator speech and résumé writing will follow in the next chapter.

♛ NOTE--- If you're a recent graduate, you'll most likely have a good idea already, but you can also ask those you are close to, "What do you see me be being good at?" and "What kind of work do you think I would enjoy?"

THE LONG-TERM VIEW

To make yourself a well-rounded employee, it's best to vary the positions you take along your career trajectory a bit. In other words, avoid the typical vertical mindset of rising up the ladder taking each successive senior position. If your background and what you can bring to the table in a new position vary but have a common thread, you are more valuable. Take me, for example.

Through the years I've worked in positions where I've gained experience with not only marketing but video production, copywriting, digital printing, customer service, project management, and graphic design. Then, add to that my side hobbies of website design, international travel, book writing, volunteer work, and music/audio production, and voila! I have a broad skill set that makes me a perfect fit in a range of different fields.

Here's another thought. Bill Sheridan, a market research and analysis chief for Amtrack, suggests that instead of changing companies, employees should move up the ladder by seeking positions within their current company but in other departments. This way, they increase their value to the company.[2]

Obviously, you'll want to be able to explain each of the positions you list on your résumé. Think through your decisions carefully. And assuming your profession is a good match for you, you'll want to keep the jobs you take within a consistent range. In other words, if you bounce around from painter to accountant to teacher to zookeeper, your résumé or application will most likely be dismissed. You'll end up appearing like you don't know what you want to do and would leave a prospective employer after a short time for something different. So why would they want to invest in developing you? Watch duration as well. Working somewhere 3 years is a good minimum rule of thumb at any position.

♛ NOTE--- See this article for recommendations on the best job search mobile apps http://bit.ly/jbmoapps

CHOOSE WISELY

Make sure you know what you're really getting into. What is the projection for the line of work you're considering over the next 5-15 years? What skills are important to have? Do you need to seek training, more education, or a certification? What personality type is the best fit for this line of work, and is that yours? Is this field becoming obsolete? If so, how can you adapt to stay in a related field? How can you parlay this position into your next one?

APPROACH

Similar to a good retirement strategy, you'll want to use a blend of different approaches. Be more *proactive* (networking, targeted networking—which we'll cover—and direct-marketing yourself) than *reactive* (responding to postings at job board sites, relying on recruiters, or waiting for anyone to email you after seeing your LinkedIn profile). Also, some people find it helpful to have a search buddy—a friend who's also in transition. You could meet regularly to swap strategies, resources, successes, and mainly just to keep each other accountable and encouraged.

♛ NOTE--- Sites to explore:
• www.bls.gov/oco - Here, you can find out more about the type of positions you're seeking—things like median salary, required education, growth rate, and projected number of new jobs in your field over the next 10 years. There is also a wealth of other job information.
• www.acinet.org - This site can display information such as salaries, trends, and education required by the state you choose.

RECAP:

1. Maintain a positive attitude.
2. Decide what type of role you want and what type of job you need.
3. Figure out what you love to do.
4. Consider an aptitude test.
5. The best career path isn't necessarily a straight line. Choose wisely by doing some research on the fields and positions you're considering.
6. Be a proactive job seeker.
7. Consider a search buddy.

Other Reading:

- "4 Ways to Improve Your Success in a Long Distance Job Search" (http://bit.ly/1BB6Noh) by Ellis Chase
- *The 7 Habits of Highly Effective People* by Steven Covey
- *How to Get What You Want and Want What You Have* by John Gray
- *Getting a Job You LOVE During a Tough Economy* by Bill Guy
- *Be Employed When You Graduate* by Jonathan Blake Huer
- *Get Top $$$ In a Job You Love* by Bill Karlson
- *Guerrilla Marketing for Job Hunters* by Dave Perry

Endnotes

1. Michael Krauss, "Authenticity: One Ad Man's View," *Marketing News*, (November, 2013): 29.
2. "On the Job," *Marketing News*, (October, 2014): 59.

3

Action!
Creating a Strategic Job Search Action Plan

MAKING A PLAN

You'll find such a great wealth of information during your job search that you absolutely need an Action Plan to help you focus—a structure in which to process all the resources you'll find. Taking the time to research and prepare is worth it, even though you may be tempted to hit the online job boards first, hard, and fast! Furthermore, a plan will help you use your time effectively and stay on track accomplishing the things that will help you get the job you're seeking.

Make, or—if you have an existing plan—update your Action Plan. You can use the sample in this chapter as a reference. A downloadable copy is available in the zip file online (www.kurt-kirton.com/hthtfiles.zip). More detail on each item in the plan will follow. You may also want to have a career coach, life coach, or job search professional evaluate your Action Plan before implementing it. You'll want to evaluate your progress and modify your Action Plan as you work through it, network, and learn more about your industry.

ACTION PLAN

<u>Goals</u>: Secure a full-time marketing management, creative services, or graphic design job in a stable industry, working with internal customers (not the public) at a for-profit company not in healthcare or music business with <15% travel, $50k+/year salary + benefits, within 5 miles of my home by ___ (date)

<u>Relocate</u>: No

<u>Job Titles</u>: Project Manager, Product Manager, Marketing Manager, Creative Services Manager, Graphic Designer

<u>Direction</u>: Seek my ideal job until ___ (a date 5 months from the date you began your search); thereafter, seek B jobs until ___ (a date 3-4 months from the last one), then C jobs with a salary of $35k+/year. Get up daily at 8 a.m. Job search/network: 9:30 a.m.-3 p.m. Read: 3-3:30 p.m. M-F. Gym: 3:30-4:30 p.m. M-Th.)

<u>Focus</u>: Doing the action items below to achieve my goals.

NOTE: Take a few minutes out of your day to find positivity, and you will find yourself having less stress and more of an open mind towards your job hunt. Think of this transition as an adventure, and remember all those who are supporting you. Be thankful as opportunities arise and things go well.

<u>3 Strengths/Unique Selling Points About Me</u>:
- Highly productive…
- Managerial-level organization skills and experience…
- Seasoned writer…

<u>B- & C-Level Job Options</u>:
A B-level job is one that would be acceptable and somewhat related to your chosen field. The accompanying salary may not quite be what you want, however. A C-level job is a survival-mode job that you must secure in order to keep your bills paid and probably continue looking for an A or B-level position. Keep track of these ideas here.

Action Items:

1.	(If you're recently unemployed) File for your unemployment benefits, and come up with a new budget.
2.	Watch or read *The Secret*. Consider doing a career assessment.
3.	Set up regular reminders in your calendar such as: **Daily** Read (Marketing News magazine, www.underconsideration.com/brandnew, www.sethgodin.typepad.com, www.prdaily.com) **Weekly** • Certify for unemployment pay. • Apply for 3 jobs (or whatever the minimum is for your state.) • Post a helpful update to your LinkedIn wall—for example, events, articles, or job openings. Also see the WEEKLY REMINDER example in this section.*

	Monthly • Decide which networking mixers to attend next month. • Every other month on a Friday, post a reminder about your job search to your Facebook and LinkedIn walls. If you're a Twitter user, tweet a shortened version. **One-off Dates** – From the Action Plan's Direction section above, log in your calendar the dates you need to reevaluate and possibly move to your next alternate choice for positions. One-offs include any other important dates that are crucial to remember. Here's an example of what I put in the Notes section of my recurring electronic calendar reminder: *WEEKLY REMINDER: **Every Monday**: • Log in, and run a search to peruse new job postings at www.creativegroup.com • Check Craigslist and www.monster.com for job postings • 2nd & 4th Mondays, see: AAF (professional association: American Advertising Federation) board www.aafnashville.com/jobs, http://part-time.jobs.net, www.nashvillechamber.com, and https://beta.governmentjobs.com • 1st & 3rd Mondays, check: Career Transition Group's LinkedIn Group http://www.linkedin.com/groups?jobs=&gid=881437&trk=anet_ug_jobs and Vanderbilt's site https://vanderbilt.taleo.net/careersection/.vu_cs/mysearches.ftl Other job postings resources: • www.simplyhired.com • www.jobalot.com • My target companies' websites
4.	If you don't have the staff at an outplacement agency (this is sometimes a perk in a severance package) as a resource, establish a relationship with a career coach at your local Department of Labor or a recommended life coach. Watch a video online to brush up on how LinkedIn currently works.
5.	Update: Elevator speech, exit statement, html/online résumé, LinkedIn profile, online portfolio, references page, résumé, SARs sheet, and Strengths/Questions/Tell Me About Yourself sheet. These will be explained in more detail later in this chapter.
6.	Sct up folders on your computer. Create or update and assemble all template/script files. Gather supplies, etc.
7.	Print some résumés and business cards.
8.	Change your LinkedIn headline and check your preferences. Post to your LinkedIn groups that you are available for work and what type of position you're seeking.
9.	Make your Target Companies List.
10.	Get recommendations; then request meetings with 2-3 headhunters.
11.	Create and then begin using your 2 spreadsheets (Job Search Log and Networking Log/Target Company List) and scripts/templates (in the Appendix) to begin networking and tracking progress.

12.	Set up or reactivate (or turn off filters that automatically trash) job posting alerts from www.indeed.com and a few top individual sites like www.beyond.com or www.glassdoor.com. If your city has a career transition group with regular job postings emails—be it through their LinkedIn group, Yahoo groups, or just email messages—subscribe to it.
13.	Update your résumé at Indeed, Careerbuilder, your outplacement service's site (for example www.righteverywhere.com) if you have one—and while you're at each site, update your profile. Also, update your profile on any recruiter sites you've joined, such as www.creativegroup.com.
14.	Post your résumé and set up a job filter at any association sites so you get alerts by email about jobs that fit your criteria as they're posted.
15.	Invite some of your closest colleagues to lunch. Start the targeted networking process (which we'll cover in a later chapter). Compile a list of regular networking events. Use Facebook or email to alert your friends of your job search.
16.	Stay abreast of news and trends in your industry.
17.	Volunteer with an association in your field.
18.	Volunteer occasionally with events that have to do with your field (ex.: PodCamp, BarCamp.)
19.	If you have time, supplement your networking efforts and get your mind off yourself by volunteering a few times a month with a local organization of your choice.

THE ACTION PLAN: PUTTING TOGETHER A STRATEGIC JOB SEARCH

GOALS

In this section, list your goals. A goal is a dream with a deadline and a plan of how to get there. It should be attainable, identifiable, and measurable. Consider whether you'd like to remain in your current city or move to a new place. If you are open to moving, determine how far you'd move, what cities you'd consider, and how long a commute you'd be willing to accept. What's your timeline for planning and facilitating the move?

Do you need to seek training? If so, this should be included in your goals. My friend Drew Dunlop once said, "What you want the employer to believe about you, you must believe about yourself." Reaching that level of confidence may sometimes require some training. Take me, for example. I never felt fully confident as a graphic designer until I learned what I thought I needed to know about Adobe Illustrator—and I became even more confident after I was Adobe Certified on Photoshop and InDesign.

What programs do you need to brush up on or learn? See if your local Department of Labor, library, YMCA, or YWCA can connect you with what you need or if you can find low-cost or free courses online. New Horizons and other learning centers around the country allow users to take classes on a number of subjects such as Photoshop, InDesign, Word, Excel, PowerPoint, SharePoint, etc. And (at least at the time of this book's writing) because of a government grant, qualifying applicants frequently can participate at no cost through New Horizons' partnership with local Departments of Labor.

JOB TITLES

Research and list some clear job titles for the positions you'll be targeting. You can enter keywords at Monster or Careerbuilder to pull up job descriptions; then, peruse current jobs that are a good fit for you. Mentioning potential job titles you're interested in will help when people ask about what you want to do. Just think if you asked someone in transition at a networking mixer what they're looking for, and they only said, "Something in education." So, identify the top 3 job titles from your list, and answer with those when someone asks.

DIRECTION

If you're in transition, decide what time you'll get up each day, and stick to it (or get up earlier!). State what days you'll be attending to your physical fitness. Decide how long you'll look for your ideal position before opening up the scope of your search to include your alternate ideas for work (Bs and Cs.) What's the bare minimum wage or salary you'll consider? Last, build in about 30 minutes several days a week to read online or printed material covering news in your field.

FOCUS AND OPINIONS

You'll find that many people you talk to—be they networking colleagues, headhunters, friends, family, or even your career coach—will have opinions about your résumé, what you should do, or how your job search should go. Be open to suggestion, but remember that you know yourself, your skills, and your education best. Evaluate the advice, but make your own decisions. Hold to your plan fairly closely so you don't lose focus or sacrifice productivity trying to chase every idea someone lobs at you. If you feel good about a suggestion or idea, work it into your Action Plan.

♛ NOTE--- If you're not currently working full-time, you may choose to seek out freelance work to generate some income. Besides keeping an ear out during your networking, there are several websites that can connect you with some prospective customers. Keep in mind that some of these sites have fees or limitations on how often you can bid on a job if you're not a paying member. See www.3desk.com, www.elance.com, www. fiverr.com, www.guru.com, and www.odesk.com. Also check out www.thumbtack.com (local focus) and www.gianthydra.com (crowdsourcing.)

Freelance work has its benefits—competitive contractor pay rate, flexibility, the opportunity to work from home (usually), helping you narrow your focus or figure out what you do and don't want to do, ongoing visibility and continuity in your field, keeping your skills sharp—and it often leads to a full-time job.[1]

STRENGTHS

Later in this chapter (Action Item 5), we'll cover making the Strengths/Questions/Tell Me About Yourself sheet, so you can just copy your top 3 unique strengths or selling points from there into this section of the Action Plan. Also, if you use or create a functional résumé (example at http://bit.ly/funcres), you can reference the Selected Accomplishments section on it for ideas. List things that are fairly unique to you so you'll stand out from everyone else naming off typical attributes.

B AND C JOBS

As much as one likes to have faith that he or she will get that perfect job, it still doesn't hurt to keep track of alternate ideas for work as you think of them—and you will come across them during your job search. Keep track of these in this section of your Action Plan. They'll be ideas for jobs you'll consider if you've not landed an A-level job by the time you set in your Goals. I like to allow myself 4-5 months to work on A-level jobs before considering Bs and then Cs, allotting 3 or so months for each of those.

ACTION ITEMS

1. BUDGETING

See Chapter 1 for information on getting your unemployment benefits filed and working up a temporary budget.

2. *THE SECRET* AND CAREER ASSESSMENTS

Some people may poo-poo the philosophy of *The Secret* (see http://nflx.it/1tIeDq4 about the DVD, or http://bit.ly/scrtbook for the book), but it has changed my mindset. It's a great way to lift yourself out of any pity party you may be having. In a nutshell, it's about the power of positive thinking combined with defining what you want and picturing how you'll feel with the end result. If you've never seen or read about this, I encourage you to give it a shot. Some interesting additional video clips are available at http://bit.ly/1tPXoEX (*The Secret* experts discuss more about the video on The Oprah Winfrey Show.) See Chapter 2 for more information about career assessments.

3. CALENDAR REMINDERS

Using a calendar can have a huge positive impact on your job search—not to mention your social life! Make the recurrent calendar entries noted in this section of the Action Items list. Ignore the unemployment-related items if they're not applicable to your search.

Daily

Make reading part of your day (or at least read a couple of times a week), so you can keep up with news in your field. I prefer to read later in the day, when my mind is tired and I need a change of pace. Your reading should include websites with news in your field, a recent book or a magazine on your field, and maybe another resource on a career transition topic. Ask around, or search the web for some top publications, ongoing blogs, or current online articles.

And speaking of reading, if you run across a term in, for instance, a job description, that you're unfamiliar with, look it up. It may come up in an interview or networking meeting, and if you understand it, you'll look more informed or intelligent! Being informed about developments and the current state of your industry is another part of maintaining value—to those with whom you network and to potential employers.

At this point you may be weary of hearing about LinkedIn, but it is such a valuable tool for your job search. Try to watch your LinkedIn "wall"—the main page you see after you log in—regularly to see what your colleagues are posting since sometimes they may post job openings there.

Let's say you hear that Bill Smith posted a job to his wall that you're interested in. Go to Bill's LinkedIn profile and with one click, you can see what he's recently shared, written, or engaged with across LinkedIn. To do so, simply look for the small triangle next to "Endorse." Clicking this will bring up a drop-down menu from which you should select "View Recent Activity." Each post will show how many days ago it was posted. Check out my profile as a good example.

Weekly

There are some valuable job postings sites that don't have a email alert system, so check their current postings at least weekly. Craigslist, surprisingly enough, is a good resource—as well as Monster, since Indeed seems to omit Monster's listings. And speaking of Indeed, there are tons of job posting websites, so instead of trying to search or set up job alerts for all of them, use Indeed. It is an aggregator that draws upon most of the popular job posting websites. At Indeed, you can set up alerts or once a week simply click the "Postings In The Last 7 Days" link in the latest Indeed email to peruse new job openings.

On alternating days—I prefer Mondays—check the job boards at association websites, your local Chamber of Commerce's website, https://beta.governmentjobs.com, and the websites of your top target companies. You can also use the following 2 sites to research associations relevant to your interests: www.weddles.com/associations and http://bit.ly/1AzejjI.

Posting something helpful to your network on LinkedIn (using the "Share an Update" field on your LinkedIn home page) will make it show up on the main page (wall) of each of your connections, just like at Facebook. This will help keep you in the minds of your colleagues who use LinkedIn regularly and can also show you are keeping up with news in your field. Besides helping out others who are interested in the content you post (my friend Erin once told me, "I would have forgotten our monthly marketing association mixer except that I saw your post about it at LinkedIn today."), recruiters or hiring managers may run across you because of your efforts. This is also a perfect spot, in addition to Twitter, to relay great job postings you want to pass on.

♛ NOTE--- If you're using your Twitter account professionally, remember that everyone can see the list of who you follow. So if you're following anyone racy, wild, or that you wouldn't want a potential employer or networking colleague to see, create a separate professional Twitter account, and add a link there to your LinkedIn profile.

Monthly

Always back up your documents (such as cover letters, job search spreadsheets, and the other documents we'll cover in this book) at least monthly—ideally to a separate hard drive, a memory key/flash drive, or Google Drive. Carefully delete all the folders in your backup space and replace them with the copies from your hard drive. This method will help you avoid multiple copies of documents where you've changed the file or folder name. It will also simplify the backing-up process and ensure you have a copy of these important documents in case of theft or damage to your computer. Backing up regularly is especially crucial for you laptop users, since laptops are more susceptible to calamity.

As far as monthly networking mixers, if you live in a decent-sized city, you could probably attend a different networking event every night! Attending these is also very handy if you're in sales/business development or are an entrepreneur building your clientele or staff. Attend any that you feel will be helpful to your search. At the end of each month, add those you want to attend next month to your calendar. But don't feel like you must attend every event; that can lead to burnout.

Job Posting Resources

Although upwards of 45% of people get their job through networking, here are some websites you can use to keep an eye out for your target positions.

- If you're a new grad, or about to be, use the Career Services Center at your college. Sometimes hiring companies will post job openings there. Employers may also seek candidates by academic department. Check with your respective department about this.

- Again, pay attention to your LinkedIn wall each time you log on. You may see a job in which you're interested that one of your connections has posted.
- Your local Chamber of Commerce may have a job postings section.
- Indeed - This aggregator site sends you listings based on the filter you set up. It references many companies' job postings as well as plenty of other job postings websites so you don't have to check them all.
- Simplyhired.com - Another good aggregator with more robust filters than Indeed. One of the largest and highest ranked job boards in the world, Simplyhired may produce job results you can't find anywhere else.
- Beyond.com - This one has had some good, solid job postings. Set up a filter so it can email you regular listings of jobs that match your criteria.
- If your top target companies have a "Careers" or "Work With Us" type page, keep an eye on the jobs posted there, just in case Indeed is not including them.
- Check out www.jobalot.com, www.jobtarget.com, or www.findtherightjob.com.
- If you're in the US and okay with the commute, you can use Craigslist to search for jobs in your nearest large city. When applying to a Craigslist job posting, always use a subject line stating the job for which you're applying, for example, "The right candidate for the Nurse Practitioner position." Employers may have several jobs posted throughout different sections of Craigslist, so including the job title in the subject line will help them match you with that position. Here's another reason to consider including Craigslist in your job search efforts: Employers who list job openings are now charged $25 apiece, so the quality of the ads has come up compared to years ago when these postings were free.
- Professional associations - Local chapter sites (for instance, the American Advertising Federation or the American Marketing Association) may list job openings and allow you to post your résumé. Check the websites of the relevant organizations in your field near your target city. Attend their mixers or meetings to network with others in your field. Frequently, attendees will hear of job openings or know someone who's hiring. (Heck, *they* might be hiring!) If you're not keen on the membership fee, check to see if they hold events that are free and open to the public.
- Job fairs - A lot of people may feel that job fairs are for entry-level or unskilled positions, but you never know what kind of positive connection you'll make! Keep an ear out for these as you network. Get on the events email list with your local Department of Labor and Workforce Development since they usually e-blast about these. Even if you don't find a job you're interested in, you may meet someone or find a resource that is of great help to you. For example, at a summer job fair, I found out about the grant I mentioned earlier through which I took Adobe classes at no charge at New Horizons Learning Center!
- If you live in or near a big city, you can network at your university's alumni chapter meetings. Surf the web to see how you can get on their email events list.

- Facebook - Personally, I have not found Facebook Groups very helpful, but you can try perusing them (use the Search blank at http://on.fb.me/1vVhJpd) and Facebook's Social Jobs section (http://on.fb.me/1x9gKaC), which includes job postings from Monster, BranchOut, DirectEmployers Association, Work4Labs, and JobVite). You can also potentially find jobs by liking the Fan pages of the companies on your Target Companies List (which we'll discuss soon).

4. CAREER PROFESSIONALS AND LINKEDIN WEBINAR

LinkedIn, as I'm sure you've figured out by now, is a valuable resource for not only job seekers but recruiters, HR managers, and those who are hiring. Like Facebook, LinkedIn occasionally modifies its website. If you feel like you're behind on how LinkedIn is currently working, review an online webinar such as http://linkd.in/1xcKFw6, as a refresher.

Establish a relationship with a career coach at your local Department of Labor or a life coach. It is very helpful to have access to an expert on career transition topics who can answer questions, give feedback, make recommendations, and provide help in person.

5. DOCUMENTS TO UPDATE

This section will have several sub-sections, so the images that appear at the beginning of each will serve as guides to where you are in the content being covered.

Item 5 - Documents to Update or Create

Actions Items:	
	10. Headhunters
1. Unemployment benefits & budget	11. Begin networking.
2. *The Secret* and career assessments	12. Creating job posting alerts
3. Calendar reminders	13. Updating résumé at job websites
4. Career coach and LinkedIn review	14. Association websites
5. Documents to update or create	15. Begin targeted networking; alert friends.
6. Folders, templates, scripts, and signature	16. Keep up with industry news.
7. Résumés and business cards	17. ... with an association.
8. LinkedIn: headline, preferences, group post	18. Volunteer with ...
9. Target Companies List	19. Volunteer in your community.

Elevator Speech

Elevator Speech

Before you even start updating your résumé, it's crucial you craft (or update) your elevator speech. An elevator speech is a brief summary that should cover who you are as a professional—your background, your top strengths, and the type of position you're seeking. The idea is that if someone in an elevator asked what you did, you'd have about 15-30 seconds to sum it all up. If you were laid off or fired, that should be downplayed. It's not really important to include the company you worked for most recently or why you're no longer there.

In this day and age, nearly everyone you know has probably been laid off at least once in the recent past. Focus more on your value and the top job titles you're seeking rather than what happened with your last company. As mentioned earlier in this chapter, providing people some solid job titles (and making sure those are on your business cards which we'll cover soon) can get them thinking about how they might help you or if they've heard of any job openings that match your interests. Here's an example:

My background is in project management and marketing or creative services work. I've been successful coordinating people and establishing procedure to complete projects as well as creating written, graphic, or web content. I'm currently seeking a marketing or project management job or graphic design position.

Short, sweet, and to the point. Once you and your career coach have your elevator speech perfected, I suggest keeping a small printout of it in your wallet or purse. This way it'll be handy in case you need to review it. On the back, I like to include the 2 main responses to job offers, which we'll cover in Chapter 7.

Item 5 - Documents to Update or Create

Actions Items:	
1. Unemployment benefits & budget	10. Headhunters
2. *The Secret* and career assessments	11. Begin networking.
3. Calendar reminders	12. Creating job posting alerts
4. Career coach and LinkedIn review	13. Updating résumé at job websites
5. Documents to update or create	14. Association websites
6. Folders, templates, scripts, and	15. Begin targeted networking; alert friends.
7. Résumés and business cards	16. Keep up with industry news.
8. LinkedIn: headline, preferences, group post	17. ... with an association.
9. Target Companies List	18. Volunteer with ...
	19. Volunteer in your community.

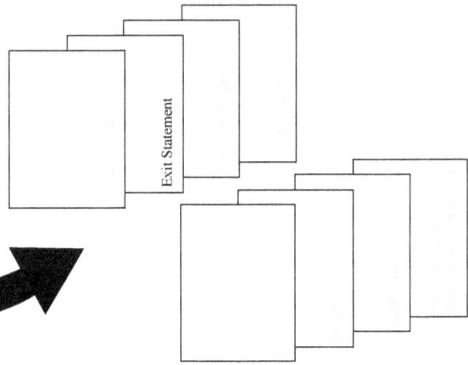

Exit Statement

Exit Statement

An exit statement is a carefully crafted explanation of why you left a job. It will come in handy when you speak with people you know or are probed by interviewers. It can cover something as simple as a situation where your last employer reduced staff as part of a recent restructuring. Or you may have a sensitive balancing act to do between not bad-mouthing your former employer while not besmirching your abilities or decision-making skills—or explaining why you only worked for the company 4 months.

If you are currently working but seeking a new job, your exit statement will probably need to cover why you want to leave your current employer, which can be a delicate situation, too. So create an explanation for this in case it comes up.

As you draft your exit statement, think about the following.[2]

- Points you want to include

- Business or industry conditions
- Impact on your position
- Your perspective on the situation
- Your focus going forward

Your career coach, outplacement service rep, or life coach can help you write this. Here's an example to get you thinking:

Like so many companies today, mine underwent a restructuring, which meant elimination of several positions, including mine. I am proud of the contributions I made at ABC Company, such as creating a social media campaign manual and the landing of the XYZ account, and I look forward to putting my strengths and experience to work in a new setting.

Item 5 - Documents to Update or Create

Actions Items:	
1. Unemployment benefits & budget	10. Headhunters
2. *The Secret* and career assessments	11. Begin networking.
3. Calendar reminders	12. Creating job posting alerts
4. Career coach and LinkedIn review	13. Updating résumé at job websites
5. Documents to update or create	14. Association websites
6. Folders, templates, scripts, and	15. Begin targeted networking; alert friends.
7. Résumés and business cards	16. Keep up with industry news.
8. LinkedIn: headline, preferences, group post	18. Volunteer with	... with an association.
9. Target Companies List	19. Volunteer in your community.

LinkedIn Profile: Photo, Summary, Overall Profile, Employers, Recommendations

LinkedIn Profile and Notes About LinkedIn

It would seem like a no-brainer to have a profile on LinkedIn if you're in transition. However, I've not been able to find a LinkedIn profile at all for some people! This is not good, since LinkedIn has become an important part of having a professional online presence, making recruiters aware of you, building a network of your peers, and simply being researchable.

Employers and people with whom you'll want to connect expect to be able to find you on LinkedIn so they can learn more about you and whether you're a good fit for the jobs you're seeking. Another benefit of having a LinkedIn profile is that you may be offered an amazing higher paying position with a different company even if you're not actively seeking a new job! Yes, it does take some time to set up an effective profile, but the information below will help you do so if you don't have one or if you need to improve your existing profile.

♛ NOTE--- Paid LinkedIn subscriptions allow such things as more robust searching, further information on 3rd degree connections, and sending InMails to those with whom you are not connected. This section (and anywhere else in the book) will refer to LinkedIn only in the context of an unpaid account.

• Photo

Use a clear, professional-looking, conservative photo on your LinkedIn profile. I'd recommend that attire be at least business casual, if not formal interview attire.

• Summary

LinkedIn provides limited space in the summary section (which is at the top of your profile page), so utilize this space the best you can. I recommend including the information below, since the Summary is the first section a potential employer will see. It can also reiterate keywords searched for by headhunters and recruiters. Further, the summary can help show others the "you" you want them to know, regardless of your past positions.

1. Contact information
2. The summary paragraph from your résumé
3. 4 or 5 strengths
4. 5 or 6 selected accomplishments (your most important)
5. Software proficiencies (if relevant for the job you're seeking)
6. Seeking - This will be 2 bullet points detailing where you'd like to work and what you'd like to do. (You can remove this section after you get your new position.) Here's a sample:
   • Dallas Area Target Position: FT accounting, _____, or _____ position in a solid, ideally medium to large-sized company.
   • Sample Job Titles: _____, _____, _____, _____.

♛ NOTE--- You can manually create a bullet on a PC by using ALT key + 7 or ALT+0149—even in cgi fields or email subject lines. On a Mac, it's OPTION+8.

• Overall Profile

It's best to have your profile as fully filled out as you can or are comfortable with. LinkedIn will prompt you to fill out your profile completely. But be more concerned with building your brand and making hiring managers want to interview you than checking off LinkedIn's suggested profile elements.

Just like with your résumé, your profile should contain keywords that have to do with the jobs you're hoping to land, so use your updated résumé to create your profile. Ideally, include no more than your last 10 years of job history in order to avoid any potential age discrimination. But it's a good idea to list as many of your past positions as you feel you need to show.

Although the aforementioned summary is branding you regardless of your former job titles, if someone gave or needs to give you a LinkedIn recommendation, it must key to one of your past positions. And by the way, LinkedIn allows you to add a link or file with each job you list to show samples of your work.

Including volunteer work on your LinkedIn profile is always a plus. (You'll need to enter your volunteer positions like they were a job, not under Organizations so that recommendations can be written.) Make sure to be detailed on what you did in each position. Not only can people can see how you've been able to apply certain skill sets in those positions, but supervisors or fellow volunteers will need a job entry to connect any recommendations they write for you.

On to preferences. It is important to customize them, so do this: Click the icon or photo of yourself in the upper right of the screen>Privacy and Settings>Manage, and go through all the settings in each of the tabs at the bottom—especially those for your Wall (under Account tab>Customize the updates you see on your home page.) This will reduce clutter on your wall so you can notice job postings more easily. Also, make sure your profile is not set to "Private." If you are currently working but quietly seeking a new job, leaving your LinkedIn profile public is fine, just obviously don't make any reference in it to actively looking.

In your education section, choose the "-" for the From-To dates for each of your degrees, and don't enter the years. This will help combat age discrimination. Last, customize your public profile URL (see http://linkd.in/1EJAe4J for a how-to.) This will make it shorter, better looking, and easier for people to remember.

• Entering Your Employers

I've run across businesses that have only a very minimal entry because a former employee added a company while setting up his or her profile. Whether you are choosing how you know someone when sending a connection request or adding a job to your profile, choose your company from the dropdown if it's there or comes up in a search instead of adding a new one. This will reduce clutter in the system and group you under the correct company entry alongside former coworkers.

• LinkedIn Recommendations

Although recruiters aren't typically swayed by recommendations, you should shoot for having at least 3. They don't have to be from former supervisors; they can come from people at nonprofits where you volunteer or from former coworkers. As I mentioned earlier, you just need to have the respective job or organization listed in your profile so the person can select it when they input your recommendation. Make sure to write recommendations for those you know when they request it. LinkedIn is about relationships, and writing recommendations for someone you'd endorse "pays it forward" and can strengthen your relationship with that person.

• Contacts vs. Connections

There is difference between "contacts" and "connections" at LinkedIn: *Contacts* include all connections you've made at LinkedIn, plus contacts you've synced in from other sources such as your Gmail address book. So the total count of your contacts will be higher than your connections. *Connections* are those who've accepted your invitation to connect at LinkedIn.[3]

If you send an invitation to connect and that person has not yet accepted and has filled out this section, you can still see some of her contact info on the Contact Info tab. After she accepts your request, the Relationship tab should appear showing the date you both connected, and you will be able to see her full contact info and send InMails.

I read once that the maximum number of LinkedIn connections possible is 5,000. LinkedIn just states in its FAQ that users are allowed a reasonably large number of invitations to connect. In order to protect members from spam, the LinkedIn system "keeps watch" on those who are trying to make a lot of connections. So if you are adding legitimately, don't worry about running out of allowances for connections. It's more about the ratio of your accepted invitations vs. those that were declined or ignored during your time as a member.[4]

If the system ever caps you, you may contact LinkedIn (http://linkd.in/1qKIfzX) to request an increase; however, being granted an increase is not guaranteed.

♛ NOTE--- Being a paid or unpaid LinkedIn member will not affect how many connections you can have!

• InMails

I prefer to send emails and only use LinkedIn's InMail system as a backup for 2 reasons:

1. Your recipient may have a new email address she's not yet entered into LinkedIn. This may delay or prevent alerts that she has a new InMail message waiting.
2. Your recipient may have turned off the preference to be alerted when she has a new InMail and rarely log into LinkedIn to notice new messages.

• Growing Your Network

The more connections you have at LinkedIn, the more likely people may be to accept your request to connect. Also, the larger your network, the more 1st- and 2nd-level connections you'll have available when you're doing the targeted networking process we'll discuss in the next chapter. Shoot for having at least 25 people in your network. If you don't, begin to grow your network. I'll give you some tips in this section.

When adding someone you don't know personally but feel it important to connect with, avoid the "I Don't Know ___ (name)" option on the "How Do You Know ___ (name)" screen during the connection request process. It will not help you, since it disallows adds. Always use the most appropriate option when choosing how you know the person because, as mentioned earlier, LinkedIn monitors your ignored or deleted requests (depending on the screen you're on, LinkedIn invitations may be accepted, deleted, or ignored.) If your requests are rejected too often, you may get a warning email from LinkedIn or an option where you can't request a new connection unless you have the recipient's email address. Likewise, don't overuse the "Friend" option.

♛ NOTE--- Connections: 1st means you are directly connected with this person. 2nd means you know someone who is connected with the person. 3rd is a person who is connected to someone who's connected to someone connected to you—those with whom you're more than 1 person away from being connected.

Here are 3 main ways you can grow your network at LinkedIn:

1. Those You Know Already - After setting up your profile, invite those you know to connect. From the Connections link in the options bar at the top of most pages, choose Add Connections, and follow the process to import your email address book. LinkedIn can then suggest connections. Here's another route: A list of "People You May Know" will also show up on different screens as you use LinkedIn. Don't use the Connect quick-link, however. Make your request more personal. Go into each person's profile to send connection requests, so you can customize the message they'll see. You can also go back and add friends from high school or college.

2. Those You Meet - Add each person you meet as you network to your LinkedIn connections. Do so within 2 days so they won't forget who you are, and always mention the event where you met when customizing the wording of your connection request. (As part of the targeted networking process, you'll be requesting LinkedIn connections to people with whom you're attempting to schedule networking meetings. This will also grow your network.)

3. Group Members - This is how I grew my network from about 50 people to 200. Join LinkedIn Groups (probably no more than 8-10) that have to do with your field. (To browse Groups, use the search blank at the top of the screen, change the setting to Groups, and enter keywords.) After you've joined the group, from the top of the Groups page, click the Members link; you can only see *all* members if you're a member of the group. From their profiles, you can start to invite select people to connect. On the "How do you know ___" screen, select Groups; then choose the Group you both have in common. Your personalized message can be something like, "Hi, James. We're both members of the Music and Marketplace group here on LinkedIn. I'd like to connect with you." Participate in discussions as often as you can. This way, you may meet potential employers or people who can help you learn more about topics in your field. You can also establish yourself as a subject matter expert by contributing original material to your groups. I once got a contract position after having met a hiring manager in one of my groups.

Another benefit to growing your network is reducing 3rd-level connections. LinkedIn now withholds the last name of anyone who is a "3rd." For example, you will see "Gabriel A." instead of the full name. The larger your LinkedIn network, the more full names you'll see.

Finally, if a fellow group member has enabled the preference for "Group members may send me messages," you can send an InMail message without the requirement of being connected or having a paid LinkedIn account. To do this, click on a name from the Group Members list to bring up the profile. Then simply use the Send ___ (name) InMail button next to the Connect button.

• Keeping Your Profile Current

Make sure to update your profile information a few times a year as you change jobs and as you achieve more accomplishments at your current position. Keep your 3 backlinks current (a LinkedIn pet peeve of mine.) Backlinks are links to things like your website, portfolio, or blog that appear on your Contact tab. They are visible to LinkedIn members, but the amount of information shown depends on your connection to the user. Google will index backlinks, helping your profile turn up in searches on your name.[5]

Anytime you change one of these URLs, be sure to update it on your LinkedIn profile. People who want to know more about you will be frustrated if they get "Page Not Found" when clicking a backlink.

• Notifying Your Connections

You may have noticed that when members make certain changes to their profiles, such as adding a new job, LinkedIn's default is to send an email to their entire network. If you don't want that, do this: While editing your profile, simply look for the white box at the upper right of the screen that says "Notify your network?" and select either "Yes" or "No" before saving the changes you've made. No more trying to remember what your profile settings are, and you can now make the choice in the moment to broadcast loudly or keep things on the down low.[6]

Item 5 - Documents to Update or Create

Actions Items:	10. Headhunters
1. Unemployment benefits & budget	11. Begin networking.
2. *The Secret* and career assessments	12. Creating job posting alerts
3. Calendar reminders	13. Updating résumé at job websites
4. Career coach and LinkedIn review	14. Association websites
5. Documents to update or create	15. Begin targeted networking; alert friends.
6. Folders, templates, scripts, and supplies	16. Keep up with industry news.
7. Résumés and business cards	17. ...ith an association.
8. LinkedIn: headline, preferences, group post	18. Volunteer with...
9. Target Companies List	19. Volunteer in your community.

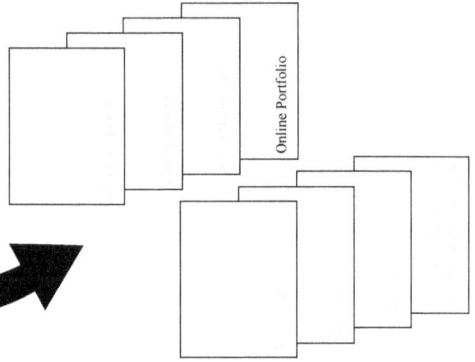

Online Portfolio

Online Portfolio

If you're a creative, you will most likely need an online portfolio during the job search process or, if you're freelancing, when pitching yourself to clients. Here are a few options:

1. If you're tech savvy, you can create a custom set of web pages for your portfolio.
2. Use www.behance.net.
3. If your portfolio is in PDF, ODP (OpenOffice Presentation Document), or PowerPoint format, you can use www.slideshare.net.
4. Scribd.com is a site where you can store documents in any of these formats: DOC, DOCX, EPUB, KEY, ODF, ODG, ODP, ODS, ODT, PDF, PPS, PPT, SXC, SXD, SXI, SXW, PPSX, PPTX, PS, RTF, TIF, TIFF, TXT, XLS, and XLSX. You can direct viewers to your Public Profile (your URL would look like this: www.scribd.com/hbertram), which will show all documents you've made Public. Or if your portfolio is contained within a single PDF, you can give out the link to just that one file.

Item 5 - Documents to Update or Create

Actions Items:	10. Headhunters
1. Unemployment benefits & budget	11. Begin networking.
2. *The Secret* and career assessments	12. Creating job posting alerts
3. Calendar reminders	13. Updating résumé at job websites
4. Career coach and LinkedIn review	14. Association websites
5. Documents to update or create	15. Begin targeted networking; alert friends.
6. Folders, templates, scripts, and supplies	16. Keep up with industry news.
7. Résumés and business cards	17. ...ith an association.
8. LinkedIn: headline, preferences, group post	18. Volunteer with...
9. Target Companies List	19. Volunteer in your community.

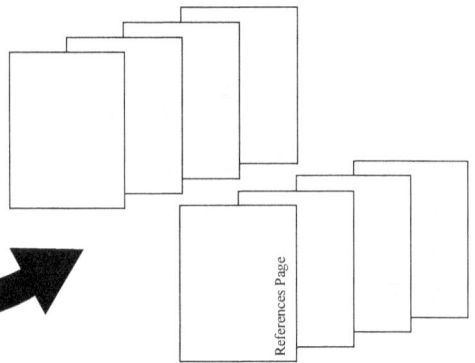

References Page

References Page

Update your References Page periodically to make sure it's still accurate. You may want to swap out some references with colleagues from a current or more recent position, and you'll want to make sure their contact information and job titles are current. The References Page should ideally list 4 people, and all of them should be professional (not personal) references.

A References Page should focus on people from your current or most recent position who (obviously!) will speak well of your character and skills. Get their approval before including them. Ask if they would consider being a reference, and let them know when they might receive a call about you—especially when you begin to get close to a job offer. In that case, you might even coach them a bit on what they should or shouldn't say or what skills of yours to play up.

Item 5 - Documents to Update or Create

Actions Items:	
	10. Headhunters
1. Unemployment benefits & budget	11. Begin networking.
2. *The Secret* and career assessments	12. Creating job posting alerts
3. Calendar reminders	13. Updating résumé at job websites
4. Career coach and LinkedIn review	14. Association websites
5. Documents to update or create	15. Begin targeted networking; alert friends.
6. Folders, templates, scripts, and supplies	16. Keep up with industry news.
7. Résumés and business cards	17. Volunteer with an association
8. LinkedIn: headline, preferences, group post	18. Volunteer.
9. Target Companies List	19. Volunteer in your community.

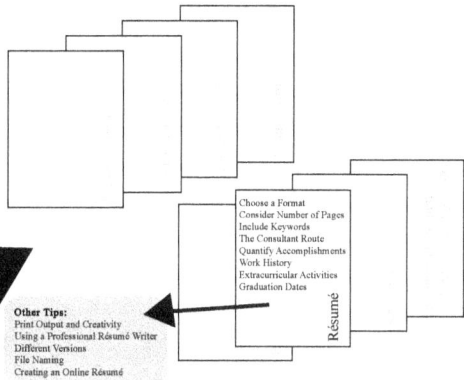

Choose a Format
Consider Number of Pages
Include Keywords
The Consultant Route
Quantify Accomplishments
Work History
Extracurricular Activities
Graduation Dates

Other Tips:
Print Output and Creativity
Using a Professional Résumé Writer
Different Versions
File Naming
Creating an Online Résumé

Résumé

Résumé

• Formats

There are 3 main formats for résumés. I won't go through these in detail since you can find plenty of great information and samples online, such as http://bit.ly/ressamp and http://bit.ly/1p1tQUz. This section will cover suggestions for finding the most effective format for your situation and tips about your résumé content.

Those with a strong work history who are not trying to change fields can use the chronological format—the most popular style. If you have large gaps between jobs, little work experience (new grad, new to the work world, etc.), or may appear to be a job-hopper, this format is not for you. A functional or combination résumé (a blend of chronological and functional) can be used if you have any of the aforementioned challenges.

The latter 2 formats can showcase your accomplishments and group your experience by skill category (for example, marketing, project management, and content creation.) Further, they can detail experience rather than just jobs, prevent duplication of job duties, and help downplay gaps in your work history or a series of short-term jobs.

♛ NOTE--- If you do have several short-term but relevant jobs in your work history you'd like to include, list the years but omit the months you began and ended those jobs.

Ah, functional résumés. When I initially considered using a functional résumé, I was concerned that it might be a red flag that I was hiding something and that the format might make it too difficult for readers to understand my work history. So I asked a headhunter, Mark Newsom of Five Chairs Talent, "Do hiring managers overlook the first part of functional résumés as fluff and just jump to the work history section?"

His response was that when it comes to résumés, the goal is to be more concerned with search engines and keyword searches, since nowadays the first step in the review process is filtering or scanning the résumés. So don't be afraid to use the functional résumé format if your background, job search, and situation call for it. A functional or combination résumé can be especially helpful if your former job titles don't match those for which you're applying or if you're changing fields. I used a functional résumé for my last two job searches and landed some amazing positions.

As far as laying out a functional résumé, your first 3 accomplishments should focus on your strongest achievements using past tense action verbs such as created, developed, or launched. Under the professional skills section, keep your action verbs in present tense—uses, develops, leads, oversees, etc.[7]

• Number of Pages

Since people change jobs more frequently these days due to layoffs, it's often difficult to restrict a résumé to the old 1- or 2-page standard. Up to 3 pages is acceptable if necessary, but make it as concise as possible. Ideally, you should try to keep your résumé to 2 pages. Just because you *can* do 3 pages doesn't mean you should.[8]

• Keywords

As mentioned earlier, when you apply online, many companies' HR systems are scanning your résumé for keywords, so research job descriptions for your top 2 or 3 dream jobs at a site like Careerbuilder for the most current skills, industry jargon, and keywords. Then, as much as possible based on your experience, work these keywords into your résumé. Include synonyms for these words throughout your résumé, too, in case the employer's filter uses a different keyword than you anticipated. This will help make your résumé "ATS (Applicant Tracking Software) friendly" and ideally get it through the first level of screening.

• The Consultant Route

There are differing opinions about referring to yourself as a "consultant" during an extended period of unemployment. Talk this over with your career coach to decide what's best for you. If you go this route, you can list your current situation as something like "Independent Consultant" with "year (the year you first went into job search mode) to Present" beside it. Under this position, list any consulting (paid or not), volunteer work, and even relevant short-term jobs. You can go even further by identifying and listing "transferable skills" used or gained during this time, including written or oral communication, leadership, teamwork, customer service, etc.

• Quantify

As you update your résumé, regardless of what format you choose, make sure to detail your *accomplishments*, not just your *duties* at each position. Use action verbs such as increased, coordinated, managed, etc., to begin each bullet point. Make sure to quantify as many statements as possible to demonstrate your value to each company. For example, "Increased productivity 20% with new tracking procedure," "Cut overhead costs by 15% in 2015," or "Raised $80,000 toward building a hospital in Haiti." As with your LinkedIn profile, keep the verbs in the description of your current job in present tense.

Frequently, accolades on your résumé are difficult to quantify—like the first one about productivity—so just do the best you can to estimate. Further, look at the accomplishments you've included, and if 10 other people could list those, too, consider including something else.

• Work History

As far as how far back to go with the positions you include, understand that you'll be more defined as an employee by the positions you've held in the last 10 years unless there's an older position that adds a totally different dimension you'd like to include when branding yourself. If you've had fewer than 3 jobs in the last 10 years, go back further. The goal is to show around 3 to 4 jobs.

If you're a student or have had meaningful internships in your recent past, list those internships in the work history section, distinguishing each from your regular jobs by explicitly listing them as an "internship."

If you've been at a company for a long time and have held several different positions, list them starting with the most current. This will show your progression through the company while keeping your job titles under the same entry. As much as possible, don't repeat duties in the bullet points accompanying each job title. For example, if project management was an element of 3 of your 4 positions, try to only list it once.

• Extracurricular Activities

You can include an extracurricular activities section on your résumé if you feel it will increase your chances for an interview and pertain to the job for which you're applying—or if you've recently finished college and need additional content. Examples would include things like volunteer work, published works, or any other relevant experience.[9]

• Education and Avoiding Age Discrimination

Unfortunately, age discrimination is still alive and well, so it never hurts to err on the side of caution. It's acceptable practice to omit graduation dates from your résumé. This can help you avoid being passed over based on your age. Additionally, don't include your birth date or a photo on your résumé. Make sure your email address does not hint at your birth year (for instance, jakesmith96@gmail.com.)

If you reach a point where you can or need to accept a job that's further down the ladder than most of your previous positions, feel free to omit some of your education on your résumé, since it will sometimes make the hiring manager think "overqualified" and immediately exclude you from consideration

Once, when I got to a desperate point and just needed *a* job, I left off my MBA. I think if I had not, I wouldn't have even gotten the interview. After a frank discussion with the general manager about not using the position as a short-term gap filler, I got the job! In most cases, I'd advise against including gap filler jobs on your résumé since you can explain the gaps during interviews. This will help maintain the integrity of your brand.

• Print Output and Creativity

Keep printed résumés on a heavy stock. Office supply and most big box general retail stores sell résumé paper. Just make sure to insert it into your printer so that you keep the watermark oriented correctly. You never know when this little bit of conscientiousness may make a difference to a decision maker! Use white or ivory stock, and keep it conservative.

If you're seeking a creative position where you feel a more innovative résumé will open doors, go for it, but keep it uncluttered and easily readable. I saw a few creative résumés in my time working for a boutique digital printing company, and being a creative myself, most *were* compelling and did grab my attention.

For any résumé—printed or PDF—avoiding typos or errors of any kind is crucial. As you finish creating your résumé, always use your program's spell check feature, but also check over the whole résumé manually. If you doubt any of the wording you've used, read it aloud. This should help you reword so the portion in question flows more smoothly.

• Using a Professional Résumé Writer

I firmly believe it's important to let a professional critique or rework your résumé. I just did this for the first time during a recent job search, and it gave me so much more peace of mind as I used my résumé with job applications, in interviews, to update my online résumé, and when tweaking my LinkedIn profile. Yes, there will most likely be a cost and it will require some extra time, but it's worth it to have a top-notch résumé in hand to complement all the hard work you're doing in your job search. Someone like Debra Ann Matthews at www.jobwinningresumes.net is a good example.

Make sure you approve any new version of your résumé before paying the writer so you can review all revisions and make sure the end result is an accurate description of you. You'll need to be able to give an example of or explain anything stated on your résumé, so if you have questions about something the professional has written, ask. If you're not able to afford a professional rework, ask your career coach for feedback after you've polished up your current résumé.

• Different Versions

You'll ideally want to have a résumé for each of the few job types you're seeking. For example, even though they're generally related in the business field, if you're seeking graphic design, marketing, or creative project management positions, it's good to have versions of your résumé tailored to each of the 3. We'll talk more about this in Chapter 5.

• File Name

As much of an afterthought as it can be, pay attention to the way you name your résumé file. Use this format: *Last name, First name-Resume*. For example: *Pitts, Belinda-Resume.doc*. This way, if a hiring manager saves the file to her desktop, it can be easily identified later. Naming it *resume.doc* is a surefire way for it to be passed over when a hiring manager needs a second look and has to go digging for it. She could have hundreds by that file name floating around!

• Online Résumé

Once you perfect your main résumé, I strongly recommend making an HTML version. In Microsoft Word under the File menu, use the "Save As Web Page" option or create an HTML document from scratch with your web page authoring program of choice. Another option for making an HTML version of your résumé is www.sites.google.com, and it provides several templates.

If you're tech savvy or have a friend who can help, for no extra charge you can host it on the web space that comes with your internet service. Most larger ISPs offer files hosting space as part of your package. Obtain the URL of the file (for example: http://home.comcast.net/~maryphillips/marypresume5-13-2015.htm), then go to a site like www.bit.ly, www.ow.ly, www.is.gd, or www.ad.fly to make a shortened customized URL for your résumé, which would look like this: *www.bit.ly/mpresume*. Be very careful when choosing a custom URL, since you may not be able to modify it later, depending on the site you use.

For an even more professional URL, if you have your own domain name and files hosting space, you can host your online résumé there, providing you with a URL like this: *www.maryphillips. com/resume.htm*. Be sure to carry any changes you make to your hard copy résumé over to your online one as well.

If you don't choose to make an HTML version of your résumé and host it on your own site, there are some other options. Not all are simple, and each website has its advantages and disadvantages.

Some, like www.visualcv.com, www.resume.com, or www.myresumeonline.org, allow you to build a résumé on their site, but I prefer to create my résumé in a word processing program to maintain more control. My goal in the following section is to recommend websites that are as easy as possible to use, keep the URL of your file the same after you make online changes (or swap to an updated version), and let your viewers easily print or download your résumé.

The free basic account at www.issuu.com displays a nice version of your résumé and meets most of my criteria, but downloading documents is not intuitive enough, and there's no print option—both of which could frustrate someone considering you for a job. After much research, these are the options I recommend along with some tips on maneuvering the respective websites. All require registration.

> **Indeed (www.indeed.com)** - You can only have 1 résumé on file at Indeed. To get started, do this: Click the arrow at the upper right of the screen near your login email address>Résumé>Upload Your Résumé. The system will parse it out, converting your document to an "Indeed Résumé"; then you can tweak each section if needed. Click the Upload button at the very bottom to post it. On the next screen, click the link to "Make it Public" if you see a warning that your résumé is private. The URL in the URL bar of your web browser on this screen is the link to your résumé. Later, if you want to replace your résumé with a revised version, make sure to use the "Delete Your Résumé" link at the lower right of the screen where you see your résumé, and—just in case—keep the file name of your résumé exactly the same as the one you're deleting. If you'd like to simply make changes to your résumé and don't see an Edit Résumé button toward the upper right of the screen where your résumé is displayed, you may need to go back to www.indeed.com and do this: At upper-right corner, click the drop-down arrow near your email address>Résumé>and then use the Edit links to change information in the section you want.

> **Careerbuilder (www.careerbuilder.com)** - You can have multiple versions of your résumé here! Upload your résumé like this: Add Résumé>Manage Résumés>Add A Résumé. To obtain the URL of the résumé you want, do this: From the Manage Résumés page, click on the title of the résumé you want, and scroll down until you see your résumé "screenshot." Above that, right-click the "Download Résumé" link, and choose Copy Link Address. (This is the URL you'll want to shorten with a site like www.bit.ly.) When you want to replace your résumé with a new version, do this: Using the same path I just mentioned, beside "Download Résumé," click "Replace Résumé," check the box for "Replace my work experience and education above with the information in this résumé attachment," then click "Save." If you

have several versions of your résumé uploaded to Careerbuilder, just make sure that you're always working with the one you intend, and never delete any résumé here that you've made a shortened link to. It's best to modify or replace a résumé in order to maintain your custom shortened URL.

Google Drive (www.drive.google.com) - Just a note: Google Docs has a separate website (www.docs.google.com) and will display your Google Drive documents, but Google Drive is a bit simpler to use. Upload your résumé like this: Click the "New" button at the upper left>Google Docs>File>Open>Upload>Select A File From Your Computer. If you don't do it like this, you can't make tweaks to your résumé later. To obtain the URL of your résumé, double-click the name of your résumé in the list of files you're keeping on Google Drive to load that document. The URL bar at the top of this screen is the link to your résumé; however, you must omit "*/edit*" at the end of the URL after copying it. As far as updating your résumé, the only option to keep the URL the same is to make your changes in Google Drive. To make changes, double-click the résumé in your list of hosted files, then begin making changes; all changes are automatically saved as you work.

Whichever site you use, you can then use the shortened URL of your online résumé when for applying for jobs online, on your business cards, and in email signatures. When applying for jobs online, simply paste the link to your online résumé into the "Paste Your Résumé Here" CGI blank. Doing so will provide the reader with a link to a better formatted, more easily readable résumé. It's also a great way to avoid carrying résumés around when you're networking, since people can easily find out more about you by viewing your online résumé. Of course, if someone gets your card and asks for a résumé, you can always email one.

Item 5 - Documents to Update or Create

Actions Items:	10. Headhunters
1. Unemployment benefits & budget	11. Begin networking.
2. *The Secret* and career assessments	12. Creating job posting alerts
3. Calendar reminders	13. Updating résumé at job websites
4. Career coach and LinkedIn review	14. Association websites
5. Documents to update or create	15. Begin targeted networking; alert friends.
6. Folders, templates, scripts, and	16. Keep up with industry news.
7. Résumés and business cards	with an association.
8. LinkedIn: headline, preferences, group post	18. Volunteer with
9. Target Companies List	19. Volunteer in your community.

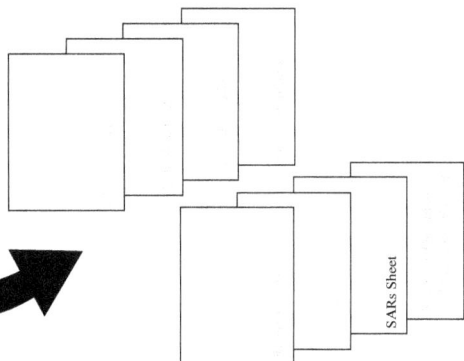

SARs Sheet

SARs Sheet

This acronym stands for Situation>Action>Result (you may sometimes see this concept called STAR, where the T is for Task.) Your past behavior is a good indicator of what you'll do in the future, so some interviewers may use the behavioral (also called situational or competency-based) approach during your interview.

SAR examples are the best way to answer behavioral interview questions. With behavioral interviewing, the interviewer asks questions designed to elicit responses from you—usually examples or stories—that will help them determine whether you have enough of the qualities the company is seeking in the right candidate.

You'd be asked questions like, "Tell me about a time when..." or "What would you say is the most complex assignment you've had, how did you handle it, and how did it turn out?" Obviously, these type questions are more of a challenge than a laid-back interview in which the interviewer asks about your last few jobs, strengths, or why you want the job.

When responding to a behavioral question, don't forget the "R" (result.) With that, you can toot your horn without sounding like a braggart by discussing a specific situation and how you made it a win. You'll want to update your SARs sheet after you leave any job, since it makes more sense for the answers to most of these questions to be examples from your most recent work.

Anticipate, list, and answer 7 to 9 of the most challenging questions you could be asked. If you're a recent college grad, draw from experiences with your volunteer work, internships, part-time jobs, classes, positions you've held with honor societies, or relevant situations with sports teams. You can search the web for many more examples of behavioral interview questions (such as at http://bit.ly/1tPYn84), but I review the set of questions or situations below and my SAR responses before any interview: [10]

- A time when I had to go above and beyond the call of duty in order to get a job done
- A time when I had too many things to do and I had to prioritize my tasks
- What is my typical way of dealing with conflict?
- A time when I used my fact-finding skills to solve a problem. Or, give an example of a time when I had to take steps to study a problem and make a decision.
- A time when I anticipated a potential problem and developed preventive measures
- The most complex assignment I ever had and my role
- Examples of experiences in a job that were satisfying and dissatisfying
- For what kind of supervisor do I work best? Give characteristics and examples.
- What are my weaknesses?

You'll never be able to anticipate every question they can throw at you. But with some practice, you can compile a key set of situations to address nearly any behavioral interview question. If you're asked something you're not prepared for, just relax, take your time, and think of the best example you can come up with. While writing this book, I had an interview where a second interviewer asked *mostly* behavioral questions.

I just thought back to my most recent jobs and talked about situations or experiences that were the best match to each question. With sensitive questions, like "Describe a time a coworker let you down and how you reacted," I spun the answers as positively as I could. Have some fun with the questions in general, and show a little personality. After all, the interviewer can't expect you to have lightning-fast answers to these type questions.

As far as the question about weaknesses, I think I've only been asked this maybe once in my career! But it never hurts to be ready for it, since it's probably the most difficult question that may come up and is better than responding with "Uhh, I don't know" or something that will dig your grave and ensure you'll never be the one they hire! I prefer to only discuss about 2 weaknesses. Here's an example: "I like a challenge and enjoy getting involved. Some people may take that as butting in, but I like to make sure the work is done right and the objective is accomplished. Without forcing my views, I think I do a good job of working in a team and leading people to the right solution."[11] Work with your career coach on how best to spin the answers.

Item 5 - Documents to Update or Create

Actions Items:	
1. Unemployment benefits & budget	10. Headhunters
2. *The Secret* and career assessments	11. Begin networking.
3. Calendar reminders	12. Creating job posting alerts
4. Career coach and LinkedIn review	13. Updating résumé at job websites
5. Documents to update or create	14. Association websites
6. Folders, templates, scripts, and	15. Begin targeted networking; alert friends.
7. Résumés and business cards	16. Keep up with industry news.
8. LinkedIn: headline, preferences, group post	___ an association.
9. Target Companies List	18. Volunteer with re
	19. Volunteer in your community.

Strengths/Questions/Tell Me About Yourself

Strengths/Questions/Tell Me About Yourself

This sheet (and the Company Info sheet which we'll cover in Chapter 6) include standard items you can pretty much expect at any interview. See both documents in the Appendix.

In the Strengths section, list your top 4 or 5 strengths in bullet-point form with explanations of each. The Goals section will have more to do with *your career as a whole* (as opposed to the Goals on the Action Plan, which deal more with *your current job search*).

Inevitably, most interviewers will ask you to tell them about yourself, be it the first thing after you sit down or on the way from the lobby to their office. Much like an elevator speech, you should craft an insightful concise response to the question, "Tell me about yourself."

Your response should be about 1-2 minutes, with the intro touching on your personal background. The middle will cover your career accomplishments and most noteworthy recent achievements. Then, conclude with what kind of opportunity you're currently seeking and why. Write up a response to this question, and practice it before any interview. This way, it sounds concise and professional and keeps you from rambling.

6. FOLDERS, FILES, AND SUPPLIES

Folders

I recommend making these 5 folders on your computer to stay organized:

1. Job Search - This is your top-level master folder and should contain the folders below plus any other files, such as aptitude tests, letters of recommendation, articles, references page, business card print files, etc.

2. Company-Specific Information - This is where you'll store information on any company for which you prepared for an interview or put in an application and can include documents you've created or information you've downloaded. You can make sub-folders by company name here and use those to file applications, directions, background check documentation, etc.

3. Core Items - This folder should contain the files you use most frequently such as your most current Action Plan, elevator speech/offer responses, exit statement, versions of your résumé, template files (which we'll discuss next), and 2 main spreadsheets.

4. Letters (cover, follow up, future position [covered in Chapter 4], and thank-you) - Keep all these letters in this folder. You can save a lot of time using them as templates, modifying them when applying for similar jobs. I suggest this format for naming the files: *Account Exec--Aug 15 ABC Enterprises.doc* (i.e., job title, month/year you applied, company). Then you can add "--fu" for follow-up, "--fp" for future position, etc., to indicate what type of letter it is. This will keep the files sorted by job title, which is best when using these letters as templates.

5. Résumés--Old - Store older versions of your résumé here. It's good to keep these, since at some point you may need to reference one to refresh your memory about some of your experiences or use the information when applying for a position that's a bit of a stretch.

Files

Here are the documents you should create or personalize. Most are provided in the Appendix and downloadable zip file. These will be very helpful as you work through your job search:

1. After I Get The Job - The list of things you need to do once you have your new job covered in Chapter 8.

2. Back Door Email - Use this script to email when contacting someone—ideally your best guess as to the hiring manager or if need be, someone else in the department—after you've applied for a job the traditional way, which is usually online. This extra step will potentially help give you a leg up getting an interview, since it shows initiative. Further, you can bypass HR, whose filters may have screened out your résumé, and/or stand out a bit more to the hiring manager when your info arrives directly from you or is forwarded by a current employee.

3. Company Info - This template is where you'll compile information about each company with which you'll interview, your questions, etc. Suggested file name syntax: *Dell-Interview Prep Info for 8-1-15 interview.doc.*

4. Headhunters, Job Search Firms, Temp Agencies Log (spreadsheet) - Keeping track of those you've looked into or used in the past will save you time in future job searches if you need to reactivate your status or as people recommend other firms. Here, you can log notes and contact info, flag those who you feel were not helpful, and assign follow-up dates. You can also log temp agencies here if they're a part of your search plans.

5. Job Search Log (spreadsheet) - This and the Networking Log/Target Companyies List (below) are your main tracking system. Some people use a notebook with a sheet of paper for each company or contact. However, I feel a spreadsheet is better, since you can quickly search for names, dates, or keywords—much less time-consuming and stressful than flipping through a hard-copy system.

6. Networking Events List - A list of networking events in your area. We'll discuss this more later.

7. Networking Meeting Request Emails - Keeping all of these in one document will expedite the writing, since you can use a previous one as a template and tweak it for future recipients. Also, as you make calls to follow up with those who haven't replied, these requests can serve as a follow-up script.

8. Networking Meeting Interview Questions - You'll find that you're able to use several staple questions in nearly every meeting. This template will also serve as a place to include contact info, meeting time and place, etc. Keep these documents to 1 page per meeting to avoid flipping through more than 1 page.

9. Networking Log/Target Companies List (spreadsheet) - *The* place to track all points of contact you make as you network. We'll discuss this more shortly, and you'll see it referred to frequently.

10. Networking Thank-You Notes - A document in which to pre-write your handwritten or emailed thank-you notes for networking meetings.

11. Older Jobs and Additional Info - Always keep a document of the details of each of your jobs and volunteer positions, logging such information as address, phone number, start and end dates, initial and ending salary figures, supervisor's name(s), company phone number, and job title. These things are typically not included on your résumé and are easy to forget. This information will come in handy if you're submitting an unemployment claim or filling out job applications. If you're a smartphone user, upload this document to Google Drive or something similar so you can easily access it whenever needed. Remember to update the version on Google Drive when you make changes to the one on your computer!

12. Passwords - Make a list of anything you use that requires a login ID and password. Anytime a job postings site or target company requires you to register, add those logins to this list. Then you can CTRL+F (or CMD+F for Mac users) to easily search by the website name for this information.

13. Recruiter First Contact Email - When a recruiter asks you to email your résumé, always include some information about the jobs you're seeking. Keeping a sample email will expedite your response to the recruiter and ensure you don't forget any pertinent information that will better identify you in their system.

14. SARs sheet - Discussed earlier.

15. Strengths, Questions, Tell Me About Yourself sheet - Discussed earlier; more information to come later in the book.

16. Working Document - Keep a .TXT document on your desktop. This way, if someone returns your call and you need to make notes, you can pull it up quickly. You can also use it to note the URLs of jobs for which you'll apply or compose short posts for your wall at LinkedIn or Facebook.

Calendars and Supplies

I've been a big calendar enthusiast ever since junior college. My progression was this: a memo pad, a daily planner, a PalmPilot, and finally a smartphone/Google Calendar. I laughed out loud at a great cartoon I saw in *The New Yorker* magazine that showed two guys talking near a water cooler. One, looking at his phone, says to the other, "I have to go. I have another coffee break on seven." While most of us are not using our calendars to get out of work when we have a job, utilizing one in your job search (along with the following resources) will definitely boost your productivity.

1. A daily calendar - Have a calendar, and use it! Include your networking meetings, mixers, doctor appointments, luncheons, webinars, training dates, and anything you'll need to plan your networking meetings around.

2. Wall calendar - This is helpful since you can look up and quickly see dates and times you are free as you set up your networking meetings. Also, list the things in #1 above.

3. Computer with printer

4. Cell phone - Obviously a land line works, too, but a cell phone makes you more accessible, which will help you avoid phone tag and frustrating those who need to reach you quickly.

5. Stamps

6. A box of thank-you cards - Use something fairly plain but professional. You can find packs of these at Wal-Mart or Target.

7. Business cards - More on this later in the book

8. Résumé paper and envelopes

9. Word processing and spreadsheet programs - Open Office (www.openoffice.org) is free to download and will export to and interface with the equivalent Microsoft programs. You can also use Google Drive, which allows you to create, open, revise, store, and export documents, spreadsheets, and several other types of files.

7. WHAT TO PRINT

Résumés

If your printer is a bit on the fritz (like mine!), or if you want really nice laser printer output, take your résumé paper to a local copy shop, and run about 5 to 10 copies of your résumé to keep on hand. Make sure the watermark is aligned properly when copying.

Business Cards

When I first heard of having business cards during a job transition, I thought, "Why? I don't *have* a job. I'm *looking* for one." And that's exactly what these will help you do. A business card is a must. It's a perfect leave-behind for someone you've met while networking and allows them to share resources, ideas, and job postings with you.

As far as content, include your name, phone numbers, email address (make sure the email address you use is professional—nothing jokey or suggestive) and the city where you're based (if you're not planning to relocate; most people will want to omit their full residential address from the card as a privacy and safety precaution), and the link to your online résumé. I suggest you not include your LinkedIn URL. Usually, it's better to have the link to your online résumé since it will always represent you better: your LinkedIn profile usually shows every job, how long you were at each, etc., which may be too much information or, for some, make you look like a job hopper.

Besides your contact information, list 3 to 4 job titles you are seeking. Again, having a few of the top job titles on your card helps people help you. They don't have to stop while you're talking and write down what you're looking for. Next to my computer, I keep a small stack of business cards from fellow job seekers I've met, which helps me rapidly find their email addresses if I run across job postings and events of interest to them.

Ideally, keep all this information on the front. You could use the back of the card to spice it up a bit more and include a fairly recent professional photo of yourself, major accomplishments, or (if you're in a creative field) images of your best design or artwork. If you plan on using images on your business card, you can use Photoshop or Google's Picasa (a free download – www.picasa.google.com) to edit and organize images. Keep the front concise, informative, and easy to read. Use uncoated stock rather than a glossy when printing, and don't have a UV coating or solid dark color on the back. All this allows people to make notes on your card.

These cards don't have to be wild or complicated, just professional. Always keep several business cards in your wallet or purse—more if you're heading to a networking event. You can design your card at an online site such as www.vistaprint.com (discussed more later in this section), or do it yourself and print locally or at home. I'd say run 150 or so, depending on when or if you're planning to change your job focus, which could negate the job titles on the card.

```
┌──────────────────────────────────────────────┐
│                                                │
│       ANGIE  HARWELL, MBA                      │
│                                                │
│                                                │
│   Marketing                      Illustration  │
│   Creative Services            Graphic Design  │
│   ──────────────────────────────────────       │
│                Shawnee, OK                     │
│   c: (580) 555-1212 • harwell@yahoo.com        │
│         Resume': http://bit.ly/ahresume        │
└──────────────────────────────────────────────┘
```

Sample Business Card

• DIY

If you're artistic and have the program, the ideal way to design your business card is in Adobe InDesign. Standard business cards are 2 x 3.5 inches. I always encourage people to make their card this size, since they'll fit into the standard business card holders in which people may store business cards they receive. Larger or smaller cards could annoy some people and easily be misplaced. If you'd still prefer a non-standard size, at least consider keeping the height at 2 inches so the card will still fit into some card holders.

If you don't have InDesign or a friend who could make your print-ready PDF, you can lay out your card in a word processor and output them on business card stock from your personal printer. Like using an Avery label—depending on the word processing program you're using—just choose Tools>Letters & Mailings> Envelopes & Labels. Then click the Options button, and in the scrollable list, choose the product number of the stock you're using (Avery 5371 is an example) and fill in the rest of the settings you'd like.

This will yield a document with a table that is set up for entering the information you want on the card. You can design it in the first cell, then copy that content to the rest. To conserve stock, do a test print first on a piece of standard paper and hold it up to your business card stock to check alignment, margins, etc. You can drag to adjust the table a bit if needed. Then print as many sheets of cards as you need. Tear at the perforations and—voila!—business cards. Regardless of the program, you'll eventually want to make changes to your card, so be sure to save the master document.

If you don't want to print your cards at home, you can send your print-ready PDF to a local digital printer. (Note: Make sure to look for *digital* printers, since they specialize in smaller runs at a lower cost than a traditional offset printer can offer.) They'll probably have a 250-card minimum, and it will cost around $100 for 250 color cards. With this option you'll most likely get to approve a hard copy proof of the card before they're printed. Before you start designing, just make sure to ask the printer how much bleed area they need (if your card will print to the edge), what file format they prefer (for example: a 1-up, high res, CMYK, PDF, or TIF), and any other specs that are important.

• Online Services

At www.vistaprint.com, www.gotprint.net, www.overnightprints.com, www.printplace.com, www.vitagraphics.net, or www.123print.com, you should be able to get 250 full-color business cards for less than $20. Some sites will allow orders of smaller quantities, and these will let you upload your own design or use a variety of design templates on file and simply enter the information you need on the card.

8. LINKEDIN

Change your "LinkedIn Headline" (the line that appears just below your name on your profile) to something like: "Project Manager with 10 Years Experience Seeking New Opportunity," and announce your job search on LinkedIn via an update (wall post) to alert your connections that you're in transition and what you're looking for. Make the "Share With" setting "Public" to reach the widest audience.

Then, post the same information to your LinkedIn groups that are local to your city or to the area in which you want to work. Use a short eye-catching subject line (like "Project Manager w/ 10 Yrs Experience Seeks Position w/ a Non-Profit in Phoenix"), and keep the content of your announcement fairly short. Here's an example:

> *Former Proctor & Gamble (name a well-known company for which you worked recently) employee here seeking project manager position with a non-profit in the greater Phoenix, AZ, area. I have additional experience in business development and purchasing. Any referrals would be greatly appreciated. Thank you. (And include your name and email address.)*

9. CREATING A TARGET COMPANIES LIST

Obviously, this is a list of companies in your area for which you'd like to work. You'll want to decide a few things before you create your list:

1. The industries or types of organizations in which you want to work
2. Size of the company you prefer
3. Ideal organization culture

Deciding whether the culture of a company fits your preference will take more time than figuring out the first 2 criteria. Culture will have to be researched online and by talking to current or recent former employees. Make your Target Companies List a part of your Networking Log/Target Companies List. See the example in the Appendix.

Make the list on the heavy side—say around 80 to 100 companies—since, as you research, you'll need to delete those that are closed or weren't a good fit. Then, group your target companies into As (your top 20), Bs, and Cs based on your interest and how much of a connection you have with someone at each company.

Besides using something like www.referenceusa.com (you'll need a library card), you can also peruse these sources for more ideas about companies you'd like to include:

- If you like the business you are (or were) in, think about your current or previous company's competitors, and as long as you are not violating a previous non-compete agreement, approach them.
- Consider the vendors and customers involved with your current or previous company. Frequently, you'll already have relationships with them.
- Search the web for the largest employers in your city of interest. If you want to work in a large city, you can also look for a directory of the area's largest employers online or at your local Chamber of Commerce, library, or entrepreneur center.
- Business journals in larger cities often publish a *Book of Lists.*
- Visit your local library, and feel free to ask for help using Dun & Bradstreet Global, LexisNexis, www.hoovers.com, and the aforementioned Reference USA website. The basic search functions should not require a subscriber fee.
- Gather suggestions from those with whom you network.
- Trade journals in your field
- And (why not!) the Yellow Pages—old school but effective

As you collect information for your Target Companies List, if a source only provides the name of the company president or owner, go ahead and fill that into the notes field on your list. Later, as you begin targeted networking, you'll learn how to identify the most appropriate person for first contact. But it's always a good idea to log the president's or owner's name if it's at your fingertips.

When a web search isn't turning up a phone number you can get through on, you can go "old school" again and pull out the phone book (White Pages). Often times, this can be an indicator of whether a company is still in business or provide you with an updated or alternate phone number.

After you've compiled your list, cross-check it against your LinkedIn connections to see if you know anyone who is working for or has worked at these companies, and enter them as the main contact for that company. If you find more than one good contact, put an asterisk by the last name of the person you've listed as the main contact, and add other contact names in the Notes field.

This way, if your ideal contact doesn't work out, you'll have others you can approach. If your LinkedIn connections don't work at the company you're targeting but are *connected* to someone who does, ask for an introduction to that person (with the goal of having a networking meeting.) Here is how to do that: http://bit.ly/rLiintro.

10. HEADHUNTERS AND RECRUITERS

There are a number of types of headhunters and recruiters, but in this section I want to cover 2 main ones. Think about them like this:

- A headhunter is an individual or employment agency that recruits candidates for various positions at companies which are their clients. There are upstanding ethical headhunters, and there are those who are less so. Some will ask you to pay for their services; others will be compensated by their client after landing you in a role at that company. You may also hear them referred to as contingent recruiters.

- A recruiter, sometimes called a retained recruiter, is an in-house staff member working for a company to fill open positions at that company.

Once upon a time, employment agencies may have actually marketed job seekers to companies. Today, they're more focused on filling the vacant positions their client companies hire them for, fitting résumés into well-defined vacant positions. Further, you may be surprised to learn that employment agencies only account for about 1.7% of the total positions found in today's marketplace.[12]

So, my advice is to seek out a few recruiting firms that specialize in your field. You'll usually find others through referrals and as you network, but be selective. Start by calling to see if they're a good match with the types of jobs you're seeking. Be prepared, positive, and professional when you call, since this interaction may be as close as you come to meeting, and your contact will form an impression of you over the phone.

Sign up if you feel the firm would be of help to you, particularly if it places people in jobs generally related to your field. (For example, they might focus on IT and accounting jobs, but they could still be useful if you're looking for a job doing website design.) When signing up, try to meet with the recruiter in person. It's likely you'll only meet them once, since most of the work they'll do with you going forward will be by phone and email.

This is your chance to make a great impression, be memorable, and help them enthusiastically pitch you to a potential employer. For in-person meetings, men should wear slacks, a long-sleeved button-down shirt, and a tie. Women should wear something fairly formal that would be appropriate in a business setting.

Whether your meeting is in person or over the phone, be well prepared so you'll come across as competent and confident. State what type of work you're seeking (part-time or full-time with some sample job titles), whether you're willing to relocate, and how far from home you'll commute. If you're asked, you can talk about your target salary range. There's no need to discuss your salary history (since you want to avoid the possibility of the recruiter poo poo'ing your persuit of a higher paying position—which I've actually experienced.) Send a thank-you note a day or two after the appointment.

Sometimes you'll find they only do business over the phone, preferring that candidates not come by. Don't worry; just email whatever information they request. (See the Appendix for a template.) Whether or not you sign up with a firm, ask if the recruiter has colleagues to whom they might refer you, or—in case it's not a match—if he or she can recommend another firm.

After getting into their system and thus on their radar, add each one to your spreadsheet of recruiters (see Appendix), and call or email your contact to check in every quarter or so. Use these agencies to supplement your core efforts. Don't sit back and rely on them for the bulk of your job opportunities. Like I've mentioned before, think of them in terms of your retirement plan where Social Security is only *part* of the big picture. Personally, I have rarely benefited from a recruiter, but your experience may differ, depending on your field.

Yes, there are still firms that ask for hundreds of dollars in fees to help connect you with the right jobs or companies. However, never pay for a recruiter. Recruiters should make their money from the employers that contract them—from having found, matched, and placed you at a company as the best candidate to meet their needs.

Whether you find your new position through a recruiter or on your own, be sure to alert all of them 90 days after you start your new job so they can flag you as inactive in their databases. I hesitate to ever say, "*Remove* me from your database," since in a few years you may want to include them as a part of your next job search.

11. NETWORKING AND DAILY ACTION ITEMS

As mentioned earlier, I recommend having 2 main spreadsheets. You'll no doubt end up with fists full of business cards, random notes, lists, and handouts, but it will be far more beneficial in the long run to add as much of this information into the appropriate spreadsheet as possible. This will help you focus on building and interacting with your contacts and stay on top of following up on job applications. The 2 spreadsheets are:

1. Job Search Log - On this spreadsheet, you'll log the jobs for which you've applied, assign follow-up dates, make notes, etc.

2. Networking Log/Target Companies List – This one is a place to track those with whom you're networking and remind you who to follow up with next. Using a spreadsheet makes for easy reference, facilitates an occasional bulk email, and provides a low-stress efficient approach to the things you need to do on a daily basis. There are other contact tracking/customer relationship management (CRM) programs available like Act! (www. act.com) if you prefer to buy one of those.

If you'd like to include your LinkedIn connections in your Networking Log, LinkedIn allows you to export your contacts. At present, here's how: From the main page go to "Connections" (at the top of any page), click the gear icon at the upper right to access "Settings," and from the upper right of the next page under Advanced Settings, click "Export LinkedIn Connections," and choose a file format. If you're importing them into a spreadsheet, use the "Microsoft Outlook .CSV" option. The resulting file can be opened with Excel or Open Office, and you'll get first and last names plus email addresses.

Use the scripts and templates included in the Appendix as you network, apply for jobs, and follow up. Prepare to discuss your interests, goals, and background as they come up during networking and interviewing. Take a look online at job descriptions for positions that mirror what you're seeking to see what key skills are currently important. Know the changes and issues your industry is facing and how you can help.

Structuring Your Day

Don't confuse *activity* with *productivity*. Simply being busy doing something for hours each day may assuage your conscience, but it won't yield the results you want. Staying on top of the key things below will make your time productive. (Note: Working on items 5 and 6 below will only last until you finish them, *not* the duration of your job search.)

1. Checking email (related to your job search)
2. Working your 2 spreadsheets
3. Accomplishing any job-search related items on your calendar
4. Searching your target companies' sites for job openings
5. Working through your Action Plan's Action Items
6. Messaging your friends (ideally individually via Facebook, since it's more personal and you'll get a better response) that you're in transition and telling them what kind of jobs you're seeking. Email those with whom you're not connected on Facebook. Open with a

bit of small talk, and try to personalize each message a bit. I recommend writing something like this:

Hi Sally,

Hope your week is off to a good start. (PERSONALIZED SENTENCE HERE such as, "It was great to see you at the Chamber of Commerce mixer last week." Or, "Billy did such a great job in the school play the other night.") Just wanted to write and touch base. I'm currently seeking

- *A full-time position*
- *In marketing, graphic design, or project management*
- *In the greater Denver area*

If you hear of anything you think I'd be interested in, please pass it along. I'll let you know when/where I land. And let me know if I can assist you in any way. Thank you very much.

Your Name
www.yoursite.com/resume.html

Before you jump into your search each day, take a minute to make a small *daily* action items list, and put those items in order. You can simply use 1 blank sheet of paper per week to write down the main things you needed to accomplish each day. The order in which you tackle them may differ, depending on what you feel is most important for that day, so prioritize based on your best judgment.

This little trick will help you focus and stay on track as you're interrupted (phone, kids, pets), distracted (the house settling, "Hey, the mail is here!"), getting anxious ("I'd rather go shopping/biking," "Man, I need a nap!"), take breaks ("My brain is about to fry!"), or leave for meetings ("Time to network!"). Not only will this give you accountability, it will keep you motivated and moving along. If you know that you'll have to bump all the dates of a certain day's action items if you decide to play hooky, you're more likely to at least get your criticals done.

Since your spreadsheets will start to get long with all the progress you're making, do a CTRL+F (or CMD+F for Mac users) search, and bold the cells with action items for that particular day, unbolding them when you've accomplished them. This way, you can see at a glance what needs attention that day. Here are some abbreviations you can use in your spreadsheets to keep entries short:

em - Email
fc - Follow-up call
fe - Follow-up email
inb - If need be
LICR - LinkedIn Connection Requested
lvm - Left voice mail
lmws - Left message with someone other than intended person

nm - Networking meeting
nmr - Networking meeting request
res/cl - Résumé and cover letter
TCL - Target Companies List
wilf - What I'm looking for
wkaeo - Will keep an ear out
wkmim - Will keep me in mind

Do your most challenging things early in the day: make follow-up calls to those you've sought networking meetings with; compose cover letters, thank-you notes, and the more elaborate emails you need to send; then do everything else.

All this probably seems like a lot, and you're only in Chapter 3, but don't be overwhelmed. In a few weeks, you'll have it down to a science! You even may find that you plateau (meaning that you work so well on your search you'll soon feel like you've run out of things to do). That's why earlier in this chapter I suggested you make your Target Companies List err on the side of being a bit too long.

Don't get frustrated or discouraged when you feel like you've been diligent at the process but you're not getting enough interviews or networking meetings. Think of this time between positions as a season, and a significant part of a growing season is planting. You are figuring out what you want to grow and foster, preparing the soil, sowing the seeds, and having a positive attitude—even though it may seem like a long time waiting for the fruit. And not all seeds fall on the perfect soil. Some fall on rocky ground, some on the path, and some among the thorns. Not every effort will directly result in a connection to that next position. But if you're faithful to the process and envision the result you want, you will get there. It's just a matter of time.

♛ NOTE--- Taxi (www.taxi.com), the online A&R agency for independent songwriters, talks about the **4 P's**: Passion, Persistence, Patience, and Professionalism. I think these are just as relevant to a job search; remember them as you go.

12. FILTERS AND ALERTS BY EMAIL

After getting my new job, instead of unsubscribing from some job postings emails (such as those sent out by networking group Nashville CABLE), I like to just make a filter that sends them to the trash. This way, all I have to do for any future job search is deactivate that filter, allowing those emails back into my email inbox immediately. Careerbuilder, Indeed, and others will allow you to deactivate your alerts as opposed to deleting them, so just turn these on or off, depending on whether you're in transition. This will save set-up time in future job searches if your ideal job criteria and keywords remain the same between this search and your next.

13. YOUR RÉSUMÉ AT THE DOT COMS

It's a good idea to keep your résumé current at Indeed, Careerbuilder, and your outplacement service's site (if you have this perk), even if you don't set up a job alert filter at these sites. Careerbuilder has more than 24 million unique visitors a month, and it works with employers around the world, including 92% of the Fortune 1000. Sometimes you'll receive emails from legitimate recruiters—usually based out of state—that are filling positions of interest to you in your city. Posting your résumé at these sites and keeping your LinkedIn profile updated will help them find you.

♛ NOTE--- If you post your résumé online (or sometimes even as a result of your LinkedIn profile), you may receive calls from recruiters asking to schedule interviews with you. Cross-reference the company with your spreadsheet, since most of these calls will be unwanted and from those you have not contacted.

14. ASSOCIATION WEBSITES

You'll also want to keep your résumé current on websites for any associations in your field (for example www.nashvilleama.org), since hiring managers may search these sites for candidates. You can always remove it once you have your new position. While you're at these association websites, set up an alert that will email you each time a company posts a new job that matches your criteria. If a particular site doesn't have this feature, add a note to your weekly calendar reminder to check that job board.

15. TARGETED NETWORKING AND NETWORKING EVENTS LIST

As often as you can afford to, invite friends and colleagues (who are close enough to your line of work) to lunch. This is an even more memorable and personable interaction than an email or Facebook message. Also, it's a great time to catch up with these people and a good way to avoid a zombie-like state in front of your computer! At this point, you'll also begin targeted networking, which we'll discuss in the next chapter.

Search the web, talk to your career coach, and start a list of local networking events (including day of the month, time span, location, RSVP information, if there's a charge, etc.). There's an example in the Appendix. Here, you can compile—in order of when they occur—all the regular mixers you've researched or heard about. Add to this list as you hear of other mixers, and try them out. Drop those that you don't feel are helpful from the list.

Frequently when we're in transition, we feel we don't have much to offer someone in return when networking. Curating and sharing this list is a good way to help anyone who's networking and have something of value to offer. And it can streamline your decision-making about which mixers you'd like to attend next month.

In regards to incorporating Facebook into your job search, I use it fairly simply. From my personal Facebook and LinkedIn accounts, I post an update about my job search every other month on a Friday, alternating between the examples below to keep it interesting. I prefer Fridays since most people are usually in a good mood about the upcoming weekend and checking their social media accounts, so I feel there's a bit more receptivity toward job search updates.

1. "Hope everyone is having a good week. Just an update on my job transition: I'm still seeking a full-time marketing or graphic design job in Nashville in case you hear of any openings. Thank you."

2. Alternate message: "Happy Friday! The job hunt is going well—I'm finding and have applied for some good positions and am continuing my networking efforts. Just a reminder: I'm still seeking introductions to recruiters and opportunities in marketing or graphic design in Nashville. Any referrals would be greatly appreciated. Thank you!"

Using Facebook and LinkedIn this way reminds your friends you need their help and lets them know you are still actively job searching. For example, my friends Stephen and Jason used their Facebook wall to announce their job searches. This put them on my radar, and I started to funnel job postings to them that were relevant to their areas of interest. Don't do one of these posts on Facebook until you've gotten through individually contacting friends via Facebook that you are seeking a new job.

16. INDUSTRY NEWS AND TRENDS

In addition to any magazines or publications that may come along with your professional organization memberships, you can also read blogs by experts in your field. Search the web, or ask colleagues in your field to identify the best ones. Subscribe to 1 or 2 of these blogs. At least once a week, read through a few entries, commenting occasionally as you have some good questions or feedback.

Try to catch the news on TV or as you're driving to stay up on current events. This will also give you something to talk about when breaking the ice at a networking event or during that potentially awkward time between the lobby and an interviewer's office. All of the above will make you more informed and help you project an air of being "in-the-know." I always say those in transition are some of the most well-informed and connected people out there, since they have more time to keep up than those working full-time.

17. VOLUNTEERING WITH AN ASSOCIATION

Yes, there are usually membership dues when joining an association in your field, but not only will membership allow you to attend all functions, in many cases, it's a prerequisite for volunteering. When volunteering, ask for a position that gets you in front of the most people. Many people find jobs through volunteering and talking to attendees. Remember to add your volunteer position to your LinkedIn profile and, if you can work it into an appropriate spot, your résumé. Other benefits of joining a professional association:

- Industry publications included with your membership
- You should be able to obtain a membership list. Add the members you're interested in having a brief networking meeting with to your Networking Log.
- If you can't figure out a target contact's email address and have to call the front desk, you can always say "It's ___ (your name) with the ___ (city) chapter of the American Advertising Federation" before asking for your contact's email address.
- When directly calling a contact who's a fellow association member, you can also preface with a statement like the one above. This is especially helpful in situations where the 2 of you have not yet met. Members frequently want to help each other or at least feel obligated to try.
- Ask your volunteer committee's leader if he or she would be willing to be a job reference, and if so, make the addition to your references page.

18. VOLUNTEERING WITH EVENTS IN YOUR FIELD

As you find out about upcoming events (like a BarCamp or PodCamp) which generally have to do with your area of interest, you can volunteer to be on the steering committee. In this role, you'll have opportunities to get to know the other committee members (who are often well-connected important people), since you'll most likely be meeting regularly for months in preparation for the event. If you'd rather not do that, at the very least, try to sign up in advance and volunteer on the day of the event. Even at this level, you can make valuable connections and have opportunities to network and share advice between presentations or during the lunch break.

19. VOLUNTEERING LOCALLY

Volunteering is important, although it is easier if you're not working full-time while seeking a new position. Not only does it help you get your mind off yourself and get *you* out of the house, it creates an opportunity to meet people who may be able to help you with your job search. Further, you can feel good about giving back to the community or making a positive impact in someone else's life. Volunteermatch.org is an aggregator that can help you browse through the current needs of organizations, nonprofits, and charities in your area.

Finally, you can help other job seekers. As I mentioned earlier in this chapter, I like to keep a stack of business cards on my desk from those I meet who are also in transition so I can forward them solid job leads when I find them.

RECAP:

- Create an Action Plan.
- Begin to work through all Action Items.

Endnotes:

1. Robert Half, "Landing your Next Job in a Tough Economy," presentation, (December, 2009) slide 9.

2. "Right Choice Search Strategy & Networking - Reason For Leaving Statement" handout, Right Management (2009): 2-3.

3. https://community.linkedin.com/questions/85113/differences-between-contacts-and-connections.html

4. http://help.linkedin.com/app/answers/detail/a_id/4800/kw/maximum+Connections+i+can+have

5. http://www.nusparkmarketing.com/2014/10/10-customized-linkedin-communication-tactics-that-will-increase-response

6. http://blog.linkedin.com/2014/07/25/so-you-think-youre-a-linkedin-profile-expert

7. Mark Newsom, owner of Five Chairs Talent, Franklin, TN (2013.)

8. Karla Ahern and Naomi Keller, "Expert Advice: Your Resume' Questions Answered," *Marketing News* (September 2014): 61.

9. Karla Ahern and Naomi Keller, "Expert Advice: Your Resume' Questions Answered," *Marketing News* (September 2014): 61.

10. Lee Hecht Harrison, "Sample Behavioral Interview Questions," *handout*, (January, 1999.)

11. Nashville Career Advancement Center, "The Most Common Tough Questions Job Interviewers Ask and How to Answer Them," *Helpful Hints for the Mature Job Seeker Participant Guide*: 9.

12. JL Kirk Associates company literature (2006.)

4

Ready, Aim, Fire
Targeted Networking

As Dave Delaney (author of *New Business Networking*) and Robert Half (founder of the well-known staffing and consulting agency by the same name) have said, the best time to build your network is before you need it—not after you're out of a job or starting a new position, such as sales, business development, or fundraising, where networking is crucial.

ACCESS THE HIDDEN JOB MARKET

A quick Google search shows that at the time of this writing, around 80% of job openings are unadvertised. Most employers, due to cost and an aversion to being overwhelmed, would rather solicit candidates through their colleagues and current employees, preferring to advertise a position only as a last resort. This is the so-called hidden job market—a place you'll want to explore. The best way to do that is by networking—and even better than networking is what I call targeted networking.

WHAT'S THE DIFFERENCE?

Now, you may be wondering about the difference between networking and targeted networking. You've always heard that most people get their jobs through networking. Recruiters, career groups, and Departments of Labor all preach this. While getting the word out to those close to you is an important part of networking, that approach needs to be supplemented. Further, targeted networking is a more productive approach than chain networking. I'll explain.

I used to network by starting with those I knew and following leads from one contact to the next, regardless of the person's field. If you've practiced this approach, you know the frustration and feelings of activity with little productivity this can cause. Yes, you're networking, but many of those with whom you talk or meet don't have connections in your field. And although you may occasionally hit the jackpot using this method, making it the extent of your networking will not be very productive. So I recommend targeted networking.

Targeted networking involves identifying key people at your target companies (whether you know them or not) and requesting an informational networking meeting with them in order to establish a relationship.

THE BENEFITS

Targeted networking is a gutsy and proactive approach, but what have you got to lose? And the best thing about targeted networking is that even if the contact you meet with can't think of anyone else with whom you should connect or companies you should look into, you now have an insider at one of your target companies. Hopefully, that person will recommend you as they hear of positions coming open. Or if you see a job listed at the company's website after you've applied online, you can respectfully ask your insider for advice or to put in a good word with the hiring manager. You'll also come away with a feel for culture as well as current inside information about the company that you can reference if you *do* get an interview in the near future.

Targeted networking will help you be more plugged in to your field in your target city. As you network more and more, you'll be able to name-drop or even help those with whom you network by recommending a vendor or partnerships with other businesses where you've networked. This will add value to your brand and showcase you as a connected go-getter. As I've said before, some of the most plugged-in people are those in transition! Folks working a full-time job usually don't have a lot of extra time or energy to go to networking mixers and be out there connecting at the level that most job seekers do.

THE PERSONAL TOUCH

An important element of targeted networking is how you meet. Face-to-face meetings trump phoners any day unless you already know the person or they insist on limiting conversation to a phone call.

When you have a personal meeting, it allows that contact to get to know you better and become comfortable with recommending you. It allows you to establish rapport, or even better, a relationship. Usually, it will make that person remember you and be more likely to help you with your requests. Let's look at the nitty gritty of the process now.

THE TARGETED NETWORKING PROCESS

1. IDENTIFY YOUR TARGET

When compiling your Target Companies List, many sources will usually display a president, CEO, owner, etc., as the main contact. Go ahead and log that person's info in the Notes field. However, top level employees are most likely too busy to have a networking meeting with you, and your chance of being ignored is high. So use the Advanced Search feature at LinkedIn to try to find someone whom you think is in a position to hire you; try to avoid reaching out to the person who has the position you want. They may feel like you're a threat to their job.

> ♛ NOTE--- When pulling up a list of employees at a target company, LinkedIn will only display a first name and last initial (e.g., Joel A.) for those who are 3rd-level connections. To overcome this, use a Boolean Google search, entering the name you found and the name of the company (for example, "Joel A" + "Widget Inc.") This should turn up the person's last name.

If you're not finding what you want with LinkedIn, surf the company's website for a staff list. If that's not available, you can call and say you're interested in more information about the company and ask for the name of one of the sales people. Don't let the receptionist transfer you to speak with him or her (since you want to go low key and connect at LinkedIn before talking), but do get a name and email address. Then, log that person into your Target Companies List as the contact.

2. CONNECT AT LINKEDIN

As I said earlier in the book, avoid using LinkedIn's quick-connect buttons on the page that will appear after you send a connection request. Connecting that way is very convenient but does not give you the option to add a personalized message to your request.

I once got a request from someone I didn't know who had barely filled out his profile. We had no mutual connections, and his request was sent without a personalized message. And if memory serves, he was from out of state. What do you think I did? Ignore. Personalized connection requests (and your relevance to the recipient) are important to getting someone to approve your request.

Send a request to connect to the target person. You will probably have to use this screen's Other option (which will require the recipient's email address, but you can use the info in the next section to obtain their email address) or Friend option (and hope they don't ignore your request), since you've most likely not worked with or met them before. If you have worked with someone, you can use the Colleague option. Remember, if the two of you are part of the same association (or LinkedIn Group), one of those options should appear, and you can choose that. Log the date you sent the request in your Networking spreadsheet.

Hopefully you've grown your network to at least 150-200 connections so that the message you send with the request can say something like, "Hi, Jason. Hope you're having a good week. Looks like we have some mutual colleagues. I'd love to connect here at LinkedIn. --Your First and Last Name" Or, "Hi, Ann. Hope you're having a good week. Gerald Carney and I were meeting yesterday, and he sent me your way. I'd love to connect here at LinkedIn. --Your First and Last Name."

When you get the email alerting you that the person at your target company accepted your LinkedIn connection request (make sure your Preference at LinkedIn is turned on for this), log the date he or she accepted in your spreadsheet. Then, you can thank them for that as part of the email you'll send to request a networking meeting.

3. FIGURE OUT THE EMAIL ADDRESS

As you log your progress with this person in your spreadsheet, find and include his email address, phone number, title, etc. as well. This will make step 4 easier. Since you know where he works and have seen his LinkedIn profile, the phone number and title should be an easy get. You can figure out almost anyone's email address as long as you know where they work. There are several ways. Here they are in order, starting with the best approach:

1. LinkedIn Contact Info Tab
It's rare that an executive will list an email address at LinkedIn, but it doesn't hurt to check. If it appears, click the Contact Info tab under the person's photo. If one is not shown, move to the next method.

2. Google
It all comes back to Google and LinkedIn, right?! With this method, you're looking for how the company's email addresses are structured. For example, jbrown@high-museum.org. So enter "*@domainname.org" where the information following the @ is the same as the company's website. Most of the time, a company's email server will be the same as its domain name. The asterisk is a character that makes the search look for email addresses that include any name at that domain name. In the search results, look for the email address of anyone at the company who's ever posted anything online. You may need to scan through 6 or 7 pages of results, since finding an address like info@high-museum.org or "customer-service@kroger.com" won't help you. You want something that looks like "tom.williams@high-museum.org" so you can see how to structure the syntax of email addresses at that company.

3. Company Website
Go to the company website's Press Releases, Public Relations, About Us, or Media Center and look for anyone's email address.

4. People Search Engines and Twitter
Try www.pipl.com, www.peekyou.com, or send your message through Twitter. Make sure your profile at Twitter is professional looking and fully filled out before messaging someone.

5. Whois.com

Go to www.whois.com, enter the company's domain (for example "amazon.com"), and when the domain shows up as "Unavailable," click the "WhoIs" link, and see if you can get the syntax based on the Registrant, Tech, or Admin email address shown there. (Note: Besides this method, the company's Facebook page or www.whitepages.com may also help you find an unlisted main phone number!)

6. Thank-You Call

Most receptionists are hesitant to disclose staff email addresses if you just cold-call and ask. If you've tried all the previous methods and still come up empty handed (by the way, you are a true bulldog if you've gotten this far!) call the main number and say, "Hi, this is ___ (your name). I'm trying to send ___ (target person) a thank-you email and forgot to get his/her email address." Who's going to thwart their coworker from getting a nice thank-you email? And also, this will help circumvent the "let me just transfer you to his/her office" response. It's not time to call yet!

7. Source Code

When you completely can't find anyone to email, there's no general email address listed at the website, and you don't want to call, but you need to include an attachment with your message, here's another idea: If the company has a Contact Us type page with fields to fill in to email them, do this: With most browsers, right-click in the negative space on the Contact Us page, and choose "View Page Source" to reveal the html code. Then, press Ctrl-F, and search for "@." Keep next'ing through until you reach the end of the page code. This may show you the company's email address. A good example of where this technique works is www.thegeneral.com/about/contact.

8. If You Have the Previous Decision-Maker's Name

When you have the previous decision-maker's name but can't find the current one, a good way to get it is to call and say, "I was trying to reach ___ (the person who previously held the position), but I see he/she's no longer with the company. What is the new person's name and email address?"

4. REQUEST THE MEETING

A few years ago, *The Harvard Business Review* mentioned that people feel more comfortable interacting with someone they've at least electronically "met." Beyond simply connecting online, it will benefit your job search to also meet face to face if at all possible, since technology will never be a better substitute for human connection.[1]

There are industries where this step may not produce a face to face meeting, but it doesn't hurt to try. You may end up being able to at least have a phone meeting. Three days after your LinkedIn connection request, send an email requesting a brief networking meeting. The main thing you want to avoid is having the recipient feel like you're asking them to hire you. In this step, you're simply interested in discussing the state of the industry, learning more about that company and the person with whom you're meeting, and getting advice on your job search. So don't be nervous in sending this initial request email.

What you'll say in each request email will be a little different since you'll know some of the people you're contacting. (As mentioned in the previous chapter, I suggest lunch with those you know over a brief networking meeting). See the Networking Meeting Request Emails document in the Appendix for a few examples of wording. As far as a subject line for this email, I recommend something creative. Here's a great article about how best to get recipients to respond to emails: http://bit.ly/emreplies. Check out the section about compelling subject lines.

5. CALL, IF NEEDED

If you don't get a reply within 4 days of your initial networking meeting request email, it's time to call! Have your Networking Meeting Request Emails document (or the email you sent) open in front of you, and use that to follow up. Generally, you'd say something like:

> *"Hi _____, this is _____; we have a mutual friend in _____. How are you today? (pause to let her speak) I'm not sure if you got my recent email, but I'm in career transition and would love to network briefly to get your advice and input (or learn more about _____ [company name]). Would you have a day next week when we could meet for 10-15 minutes or so?"*

Sometimes she may not be able or willing to have a networking meeting but will cut to the chase right then over the phone, so have your elevator speech ready and ask if she knows of anyone with whom you should connect and any companies you should be looking into.

If she's out of office, don't leave a voicemail. Instead, call once more later that day. If she's still out of office, don't leave a voicemail. Call the next day. Move to step 6.

♛ NOTE--- When someone can't or won't meet but requests your résumé so they can pass it on, make sure the email you send includes 2 or 3 top job titles in which you're interested; thank them for passing on your résumé to someone who could help; and close with your name, email address, and online résumé URL. Don't forget to attach your résumé!

6. VOICEMAIL

If your target contact is out of the office or you're still getting voicemail by your third call, go ahead and leave her a message. If you find out she is away from the office on a trip, call the day after her return date to allow her time to catch up around the office. If after 3 to 4 more days, she has not responded to your voicemail, follow the options below. When it comes to leaving a voicemail—whether it's a follow-up call regarding a networking meeting or a job for which you've applied—smile as you do it. You may feel silly, but (that'll make you smile and) it'll convey positivity and hopefully entice the recipient to return your call.

7. TWO OPTIONS

If she still won't respond, either use LinkedIn to find someone else at the company with whom to network and start the process over or drop by looking sharp with a résumé and customized cover letter addressed to the attention of the person you can best guess would be a hiring manager for a position you would want. This is where keeping up with the owner, president, VP, or CEO's name may come in handy. It's what I call the *future position drop-off*; see the sample letter in the Appendix and step 8 here for more information.

8. THE FUTURE POSITION DROP-OFF

♛ NOTE: This tactic could annoy some people, but it can also show gumption and interest. Use your judgment.

The future position letter should be addressed to the person you best surmise is the hiring manager for the position you want. If it's a small company or if you're unable to find the name of the hiring manager, address it to the owner or VP of the most relevant department. The letter should mention the title of the position you want, why you'd like to work for the company, and include a table of the typical duties for that position versus your qualifications. Close with a request to be kept in mind should such a position arise. See sample in Appendix.

Pop in to the office, ideally not too early, late, or close to the lunch hour. Men, wear nice slacks, a button down, and a tie or blazer. Ladies, dress formally but not quite as formal as you would for an interview. Ask for the person to whom you've written the cover letter. You can go 2 routes with this—which one you choose depends on your relationship with the person and what communication you've had leading up to this.

1. The bold approach - Tell the receptionist that you have not been able to reach ___ (name of the person to whom your letter is addressed) and wanted to see if she had a minute to allow you to drop off a résumé and meet you in person. If the hiring manager *does* come out and meet you, congrats! Don't hold her too long—she wasn't expecting you. Simply introduce yourself, explain that you're in transition and seeking a ___ (position), just wanted to introduce yourself, drop off a résumé, and would appreciate her keeping you in mind should such a position open. If she's not available, leave your documents with the receptionist.
2. The passive approach - You might use this one when you feel like the recipient is legitimately very busy, not interested, or that this is a last-ditch effort but you want to bring closure with this company by following through. Tell the receptionist something like, "I haven't been able to reach Sally, and I know she's been very busy. She wasn't expecting me, so I just wanted to drop off my résumé for her."

Since you're popping in unannounced, you usually will not be able to meet the hiring manager, so be sure to treat the receptionist with equal respect. Connect as best you can with this person, since (fingers crossed!) they could be your in-office advocate. Make some small talk; ask if this is a busy time of year or how their day is going. These folks have more influence than you might expect. They're usually the one hand-delivering your résumé and cover letter to the intended party and may be asked about you—your appearance, professionalism, or personality. Or they may like you enough to recommend you for the job you're seeking; at small companies, the receptionist's opinion can make a difference.

9. YEP, FOLLOW-UP CALL IF NEEDED

After a future position drop-off, if you are unable to meet the potential hiring manager, call to follow up in 4 days, introducing yourself and making sure he received your documents. And whether you got to meet the intended recipient or not, make a note in your spreadsheet to call about 6 weeks out to follow up with her about whether there are any openings. A lot can happen in 6 weeks! Follow up at least a couple of times over the next 12 to 14 weeks—by phone for the first point of contact and email for the second. And if you're having trouble getting through, try calling fairly early or late in the day, before her assistant is in or after 5:00 so she's answering her own calls.

Like I mentioned in step 7, instead of doing a future position drop-off, you can go back to your Networking Log and repeat this process with—if you have one—a different person at the company. If you don't have an alternate contact and if the company is large enough to have salespeople, you can always have a networking meeting with one of them, and then see if they can get you in touch with someone in your target department.

Last, after exhausting every appropriate contact at the company, if you still have not been able to have a networking meeting with anyone, you can always lay down the gauntlet at that point, knowing you've done all you can. I've reached this point with several companies in the greater Nashville area over the years. Note this in your Target Companies List. You may want to strike through this company as well.

If you *are* successful at any point during steps 1 through 6, schedule, prepare for, and have the networking meeting. Follow up with a thank-you card, and then email to follow up in 6 to 7 weeks to see if that person has heard of any open positions or thought of anyone else with whom you should connect.

You can use targeted networking with the people referred to you by the person you met with. Log all stages of your progress in your Networking Log/Target Companies List.

♛ NOTE--- When someone—be it someone you've had a networking meeting with or anyone you meet—asks you to email your résumé so they can keep an ear out about job leads for you, make the subject line like this: *Your Name—Résumé (seeking ___ [2 or 3 job titles here].)* This way if they run across something, they can more quickly find your résumé if they've saved your email.

THE TARGETED NETWORKING APPOINTMENTS

So your diligent targeted networking has paid off with a networking appointment—bravo! Let's go over how to prepare for and have the meeting and what to do afterwards.

Before

After you've put the reminder in your calendar (and ideally written it up on your wall calendar), know that it's also a good idea to email that person the night before or the morning of to remind them about your meeting. I like to keep their latest email in my Inbox, which I use to send the reminder, until after the meeting. This way, you prevent either one of you forgetting. You'll also want to do a bit of research on them and the company and log (on your Networking Meeting Interview Questions sheet) the time and place of your meeting along with his or her name, position, and phone number—ideally their cell phone number, if you have it, just in case you get lost, run late, or end up unable to make it.

You can use the Networking Meeting Interview Questions sheet (in the Appendix) to put together some questions, but the flow will generally be:

1. Small talk
2. (If applicable) how you know your mutual colleague or 1 or 2 people you saw that you both know on LinkedIn
3. Questions about their interests, life, etc.
4. Questions about the company
5. Your elevator speech
6. Call to action/asking for their input
7. You might want to ask if you may email your Target Companies List to see if they know anyone working at any of them.

As you prepare, see whether your target contact has worked at any of your other target companies in the past. If so, you can ask what he thought of the company and gain some insider perspective, hear whether it's a good place to work, or possibly find the right insider with whom to network. LinkedIn's "Previous" field (at the top of a profile under the name of any LinkedIn member) will provide a quick look at some of their previous employers if you'd rather not scroll through the whole profile.

If applicable, you can also break the ice by asking about 1 or 2 of your mutual LinkedIn connections. Don't ask things about the company you can easily find out from its website, such as when the company was established or what they do.

Bring your Networking Meeting Interview Questions sheet, a nice folder with a pad of paper, a pen (so you can take notes), your résumé (in case you're asked for it), and your business cards.

Dress business casual. If you've never met the person before and you're meeting somewhere other than their office, look up their photo on LinkedIn so you can spot them upon arrival.

The conversation will be more natural if you try to commit to memory your core questions from your Networking Meeting Interview Questions sheet. Then, after the meeting (say, in your car before you leave and begin to forget), fill in the answers.

During

I remember my first networking meeting. It was with someone at Outback Concerts, a company that books appearances for musicians or comedians. Around the 15-minute mark, we were still talking, and since I'd always heard it was so important to keep these meetings short (and say 10 to 15 minutes in my email request for the meeting), my instinct was to excuse myself, hop up, and go.

Resist that inclination: If it's going well and the contact doesn't seem antsy or like he needs to get going, feel free to meet more than 10 or 15 minutes. Some people will enjoy talking to you and giving you advice on your job search. The main thing is to keep it laid back and conversational, so you can make a good connection.

As you talk, only take quick notes on important pieces of information. This will help the conversation flow better—you want this to be more of an interaction than an inquisition! If you think of any resources you have that could help your contact, such as vendors, networking events, seminars, conferences, articles, etc., be sure to mention them.

Toward the end of the meeting, if you feel you've established a good rapport, you can politely ask if you may send your Target Companies List later that week to see whether he might know anyone at those companies.

Don't feel like you have to call on every contact you're given. You need to stay within your goals. But don't critique these contacts during the networking meeting (for instance you're referred to someone that wasn't helpful or at a company for which you don't want to work.)

After

Send a written thank-you note (see example in Appendix). If you don't have an address for the person and can't get one, it's appropriate to send a thank-you email. Follow through on the action items that arose from the meeting, and if the contact okay'ed it, email him your Target Companies List.

File the Networking Meeting Interview Questions sheet somewhere you can find it later, since you may use some of that information in a future interview. Add to your spreadsheet the date of the meeting, the date you sent the thank-you note, and a reminder about 6-8 weeks out to do a follow-up call or email to check with your contact and remind him that you're still looking for work. (If you've found a job, there's no need to follow up).

When you're given contacts at companies you're interested in working for, don't wait until a position comes open to meet with them. Go ahead and meet as soon as you can to establish goodwill or a relationship. This way, you come off more genuine than a last minute, "Ooo, ooo, I want this job and we both know ___, so help me!" approach. And it doesn't hurt to meet with more than one contact at your target companies if you end up being referred to several and want to invest the time.

Sometimes someone will offer help by suggesting you look through their LinkedIn connections and ask for introductions. Doing this would be useful if you're adding new companies to your Target Companies List. Unfortunately, there is not currently a way to Advance Search the connections of one of your LinkedIn colleagues. Some folks have *hundreds* of connections, and if you're only interested in those who are in your area, there's no way to display a list of those currently in your city.

So to avoid having to open each one and see where they're based, try this if you are 1st-level connected: From your contact's main LinkedIn page, click the number that shows how many connections they have. That will take you down to the connections section of their profile page. Click on the magnifying glass icon, and enter the name of the city for which you'd like to filter. This will display only those who have that city's name in their profile—who are working or have worked in that city—helping you whittle down search results somewhat.

My suggestion to improve this functionality has been sent in and acknowledged, but LinkedIn hinted that when many members request the same improvement, that's the best way to implement it. So, I'd urge you to click the feedback link on the right side of your LinkedIn homepage (or go under Help Center and click Contact Us), and suggest allowing advanced searching of members' connections. This way, users could search by company, city, *and* currently employed, resulting in a more useful list of people who are currently working for the target company in the city of their choice.

IF YOU PLATEAU

As I mentioned in the last chapter, sometimes you may feel like you've run out of things to do for your job search. If that happens:

1. Make sure you have accomplished everything on your Action Plan and are regularly checking the online job boards of your target companies.
2. Respond to more job postings.

3. Make sure you're doing some regular follow-ups with those in your network.

4. Sift back through your target companies to make sure you're on top of being in touch and have networked with at least one person at each (and moved on to someone else if your first person did not respond or would not meet).

5. Attend more networking events.

6. You can always add more companies to your Target Companies List and start to network through those.

It's worth saying again at this point: *Don't get discouraged.* Although my friend I mentioned earlier in the book seems to have nearly no down time between jobs, the season of job search is not a fast or easy one for the vast majority of us. Keep sowing your seeds. Be consistent. Allow yourself to have fun regularly. Remember, you're not the only one in career transition. Draw encouragement from others, and be an encourager as well.

ADVICE YOU RECEIVE

Temper all advice from those who weigh in on your job search (be they your spouse, friends, or family) with your own wisdom. *You* know you better than anyone. *You* have thought hard, planned, and come up with your goals, Action Plan, and Target Companies List. Be proud of your mission, adventure, and progress. Be open to receiving admonition (especially from those in your field), but don't let anyone giving you a sour face about your job search shake you. It's *your* search, and you can make any major re-evaluations or adjustments in the context of the overall process at any time.

RECAP:

• Identify the person with whom you'd like to have a networking meeting.
• Connect with that person at LinkedIn.
• Research their email address, phone number, and job title, and log them in your spreadsheet.
• Four days later, email to request a networking meeting.
• If there's no response within 3-4 days, call.
• Call twice at different times during the day if needed. Don't leave a voicemail.
• If you can't get the person, call once more the next day. Do leave a voicemail this time if you are still unable to reach him or her.
• If there's still no response after 3 more days, you can either try the process again with someone else at that company or drop off a Future Position Letter and résumé.
• If you are unable to meet the potential hiring manager during the drop-off, call to follow up in 4 days. Log all points of contact and reminders for the next step in your Networking Log.
• If you *are* successful anywhere throughout steps 1 through 7, prepare, meet, send a thank-you card, and follow up in 6 to 7 weeks.

Endnote:

1. https://hbr.org/2010/02/how-to-make-your-network-work.html

5

Go Forth
Networking Events and Applying for Jobs

Although it's the most challenging tactic, networking is the top way people get hired. In fact, 45% of hirings result from networking, which breaks down to 21% from offline networking and 24% through employee referrals.[1]

Whether your network has flourished, languished, or died on the vine, in this chapter, I'm going to cover how to breathe some new life into it and put it to work. Granted, networking—especially if you're shy or an introvert—can be intimidating. But like with most things, the more you do it, the savvier you'll become. Combine networking events and job fairs with the targeted networking we discussed in the previous chapter, and you've got a well-rounded plan for networking.

NETWORKING EVENTS AND JOB FAIRS

Remember, perception is reality when it comes to networking events, so be ready with your elevator speech, confident in your skills and how you talk about your work, pleasant, personable, and professional. Present yourself more as someone in your profession who is networking, not a job seeker.

Working a Room

Networking begins the minute you roll up in your car. You may find someone walking in, in the elevator, or waiting for someone else in the lobby heading to the same event. So be ready. Have plenty of business cards with you. If you're also there to let people know about your side business, don't bring brochures: these may be taken as too much of a sales pitch, or you may come off as pushy.

Put your name tag on your right—this is the left for everyone else. People read left to right, so this makes more sense. Many who are currently working will be writing their company name or title below their name. Feel free to leave that space blank. Sometimes this is a conversation starter prompting people to ask, "Where do you work?" Then you can respond with your elevator speech.

Nearly everyone at a networking event is there to connect with others, so don't feel overwhelmed or as if the word "NEW" has been stamped on your forehead. Most will be pleasant and welcoming, and there will be other first timers. Start by talking to 1 or 2 people you know. This is a good way to ease into the event, and these colleagues may introduce you to others you don't know. But challenge yourself, and aim to meet mostly new people.

Avoid the tendency to stand with your arms crossed. Although this may feel comfortable, it's a closed posture, and this body language will not make you approachable. Scan name tags as much as you can, looking for people who work for any companies of interest to you or in a role that could help you.

It's best to make meaningful connections with a few rather than handing your business card out like a vending machine! Remember, quality over quantity. During my first time at a regular Nashville mixer, a lady I met introduced herself and promptly laid her business card on me. I thought, "Wow; slow down. You gotta romance me a little first!" I like how one resource I read phrased it: "Demonstrate restraint." You don't want to appear desperate or push your business card at someone too early.

If you're shy or new at the job hunt, it may be intimidating to try to meet even a couple of people. But start off slowly. Have a goal to meet 3 or 4, and you may even end up talking to more.

When opening with small talk so you can work up to learning what the other person does, you can ask things like[2]:

- Have you been to this mixer before?
- How did you hear about it?
- Do you know ___ (someone on the leadership committee for the event)?
- How long have you lived in ___ (their city)?
- In what part of town do you live?
- Where are you from originally?
- Have you been to any other networking events that you found valuable?

Or you can use the old standards, like the weather, sports, traffic/parking, and industry topics. After working up to casually mentioning what you do, then ask:

- What do you do?
- Who are some of your clients?
- What do you like about your position?
- How long have you been with the company?

To get started with those you don't know, look for little groups with gaps, and ease into those. Then, during a pause, you can contribute to any conversation where you have something relevant to say. You can also look for people standing by themselves and strike up a conversation with them.

If you find someone hovering near your group or doing the "groups with gaps" approach, invite them in, taking a moment to make introductions. Another way is to stand near the entrance to the room or meeting area and start conversations after someone has checked in but before they're engrossed in other conversations.

Like with interviewing, shake hands firmly and introduce yourself. Always keep a positive attitude when you network and avoid bashing former employers or vendors. Keep your energy and enthusiasm up. Smile, and really listen instead of looking around the room at others or (as I'm sometimes guilty of) thinking about what you want to say next. Sustain eye contact, and ignore distractions. Don't give a full sales pitch for anything as you network.

Think about ways you can help the other person. Keep it natural and genuine. Then, nonchalantly and when the time feels right, ask for their card, and offer yours. Swapping cards is good not only so you can connect with them on LinkedIn or send them a prospective customer but because you may eventually think of something helpful or run across an event or article in which they might be interested. Always make notes as necessary after your conversation, such as things this person said they would do for you or people they're planning to introduce you to, things you promised to send them, the name of the event at which you met, etc. The back of their business card works best.

As you attend some of the same regular mixers, don't feel like you need to focus completely on meeting new people. It helps to acknowledge or have a few minutes of conversation with someone you know or met the last time. When they see you again and again, you'll probably be top of mind when they *do* hear about a position that fits you. Being seen also shows others that you're working hard at being out there, getting involved, and staying proactive in your job search. Some may even see you as "a bulldog," like one of my former coworkers called me! All this networking will increase your knowledge, lend to your credibility, and get you noticed for positions you're targeting.

Try not to dominate any one person's time, whether it's someone you know or not. A good conversation with one person runs around 5 minutes. Pay attention if the person becomes restless. Breaking away to do further mingling will be of value to both of you, since you'll want to make more connections. Be gracious in your exit, and thank the person. You can use reasons like those below to move on, finishing with, "It was great to meet you," "I'll send you that ___ (information you discussed)":

- I'm going to find the restroom, a trash can, etc.
- I'm going to get another drink/freshen up my coffee.
- I'm going to mingle around.
- Have you met ___? (a handoff to someone you know)

Networking is a two-way street, so as much as you are able, share information, contacts, tips, etc.—be they in regards to the person's hobbies, interests, home projects, job search, employee needs, or whatever. Then, like with targeted networking, always follow through, and send any information you promised within the next 48 hours. Schedule some coffee dates with people you'd like to talk with further.

Job Fairs

Job Fairs can be hit or miss depending on how many and which companies are participating. But if you have time, it never hurts to pop by some job fairs you feel will be worth the effort. Like having your résumé online with a few job sites or using headhunters, it doesn't hurt to diversify your job search efforts.

If you can, try to get a list of the attending companies from the organizer ahead of time. Look up the currently posted positions, and gather a little more information about each of those in which you're interested. Men, wear nice slacks, a button down shirt, and a tie or blazer. Ladies, dress formally but not quite like you would for an interview.

Try to arrive either 1 hour after the start time (to avoid being lost in the initial rush) or 30 minutes after the lunch hour (to allow the company reps/recruiters to have a lunch break). Don't wait until too close to the ending time, since some will pack up and leave early. Bring your business cards, a couple of résumés, and a notepad in a folder (like a padfolio.) This way, you'll have cards to give any fellow job seekers you end up networking with, résumés for the reps who request one, your cards as a back-up if you run out of résumés, and your notepad to take notes.

It's always good to establish some rapport with one of the recruiters at the companies in which you're interested so you can try to stand out from everyone else they'll meet. This way, down the road, you can send them your résumé after you've applied for a job. Also, it may help them remember meeting you.

Ask anything you'd like to know about any open positions that appeal to you. Stacie Garlieb of Successful Impressions suggests this: Ask about what skills top candidates for ___ (position you saw posted) need to have. Find out what a typical career path is for someone starting in that position. Then, after you've related a few examples from your experience to show why you'd be a strong candidate and expressed genuine interest in the company, ask what additional information you could provide in order to schedule a time to interview.[3]

If there aren't any positions you're currently interested in, get a business card, and thank them before you move on to the next table. After you return home, log the recruiters you met in your Networking Log/Target Companies List so you can call upon them when needed.

APPLYING FOR JOBS

Prepare

What's the old Boy Scout motto? Be prepared. That's definitely the case when it comes to doing job applications. Make sure you have completed or updated your Older Jobs and Additional Info sheet we discussed earlier in the book. (It's the document where you're logging a lot of key information about each job that may not be shown or necessary on your résumé.) You'll need this information to complete most job applications.

Using the job description or your research on the company, consider these factors as you choose which jobs to apply for:

- The fit with your job focus/target position
- Wages
- Education or training required
- Job location
- Benefits
- Environment
- Potential for advancement
- Industry growth or decline

What's the Deal?

When surfing for job openings the traditional way (through printed publications, job postings sites, or the websites of your target companies), have you ever wondered how many of these jobs are filled already...situations where the hiring manager already has the top candidate picked out? Why are they wasting our time listing jobs if this is the case? It may be a back-up in case the ideal candidate doesn't end up taking the job.

Then you may ask, "Is there a law that companies have to make job openings public?" No, it's not a law—at least with non-government jobs—but it's often a company policy. Clay Faircloth of the Nashville Career Advancement Center says it depends on the company, but large companies usually have a policy that all jobs must be posted.

Sure, there will always be a possibility that the job for which you're applying online is already essentially filled. But like I alluded to in the Job Fairs section, your job search is kind of like a good retirement strategy. You want to diversify your efforts somewhat, and being aware of job postings is an element you should include. I got my first job at a record label as a result of a blind ad in the newspaper.

Indeed

Here's something I learned about job postings from Indeed's customer support:

> Indeed.com includes all the job listings from major job boards, newspapers, associations and company career pages. The jobs contained in Indeed's search results, or linked from those results, have been created by people over whom Indeed exercises no control. Indeed's job search results are indexed in an automated manner, and Indeed is not able to screen all of the jobs on the site.

So if you feel like you've found a different helpful job postings site that Indeed doesn't seem to include, add it to your weekly calendar reminder, and check job results there as well.

If you have any doubts or reticence about a company listed on Indeed or any other job postings site, do a bit of research. You may see certain companies post the same type job week after week and wonder if they're just churning through workers. Do a Boolean search on Google, entering the company's name + "scam" to search for feedback from those who have interviewed with or previously worked for this company. Glassdoor is also a great resource for employee feedback.

Job Applications

At one position, I coordinated applications for those interested in security guard positions. In the "Why did you leave this position?" blank next to one applicant's previous fast food job, a girl wrote, "Place was robbed. I was scared." I still get a chuckle out of the honesty and brevity of her response.

As far as job applications are concerned, don't apply for a position unless you meet at least 75% of what the company is looking for, and only apply if you're seriously interested and qualified. Usually the first 5 bullet points in a job description are the most important duties.

Sometimes on an application you'll be asked about your salary requirements or history. You don't want an employer to exclude you from an interview based on either of these, since in an interview, you can explain the value you'd bring to the company and why you're worth a certain salary. If you are able, write "flexible" (not "negotiable," since "flexible" sounds a little more positive) in the "salary required" field. If an online application will not allow that, try to leave it blank. And if that's not possible, fill in a figure you feel is reasonable.

If a job posting requires that you disclose your salary expectations and you can email in your response and documents (like with Craigslist), include something like this in your cover letter or the body of your email: "As far as salary expectations, I am currently seeking a pay range ideally between $30-40k, but am more interested in the right opportunity, work of interest to me, and a company where I can make a meaningful contribution."

As far as salary *history*, if there are blanks for salary next to each of your previous jobs, try to leave those blank as well. If they force an answer, don't count any bonuses. Do include commission, and try to enter a range.

Cover Letters

It's always a good idea to include a cover letter with any résumé you send. A cover letter will help explain why you're a solid fit for the position and can relate any additional information that may not appear on your résumé.

Like me, you may wonder whether, after all your hard work crafting an eloquent cover letter, it will be completely overlooked. I once heard a recruiter say that about half of recruiters out there like or will read cover letters; the other half don't. And most filters won't scan your cover letter for keywords, only your résumé. But it's important—especially if you're changing careers—to be able to explain why you fit the requirements of the job.

Here's where a T-letter (also called matrix style) cover letter comes to the rescue. (See sample in Appendix.) The beauty of this style is that it's easy for a reader to scan and will match your qualifications with the bullet-point requirements of the job. And, because of the bullet-point format, it's easier for you to word than a traditional style cover letter. Keep verb references to your current job in present tense and those to previous jobs in past tense (e.g., managing, overseeing, designing vs. established, wrote, programmed.)

When writing cover letters, if you have any doubt that something might sound odd, read it out loud, and revise it until it sounds right. Most hiring managers will check out your cover letter. If you're applying online and the site only allows uploading a résumé (no cover letter), make a version of your résumé file where the cover letter is the first page, and upload that.

Customizing Résumés

If you've ever heard you should customize a résumé for the job for which you're applying, before you roll your eyes and think, "Ugh!" consider this route: Create a master résumé, then tweak it only for job opportunities you feel merit a customized résumé. This approach matches you with the position a bit more specifically.

You can also limit tailoring résumés only to openings at your top 10 target companies. (Customizing a résumé for *every* job you apply for can make you nuts!) I like to have a few slightly different versions of my master résumé (e.g., marketing, graphic design, project management), then I submit the one that best fits the job, using my judgment about whether or not to customize.

As far as how to customize, here are some ideas. Change your main job title; reword the summary paragraph; resequence your accomplishments or skill sections; and/or weave in keywords from a target job's description. Whether your education or technical skills section should be first or last on a chronological résumé will depend on the job description and in what you feel the employer is more interested.

I worked for a company that I heard was not good at using accurate job titles. So when I reference that position on my résumé, I use a more fitting job title. However, if you're filling out an application, you must put your *actual* job title. In that case, you can put the clarified title you use on your résumé in parentheses next to the actual title.

Salutations

When you're writing:

- A cover letter or follow-up email to a hiring manager when applying for a job, since a letter is a more formal endeavor, it's best to say, "Dear Mr. or Ms. ___ (last name)," unless you know them personally.
- An email for a networking meeting or a reminder message: it's appropriate and more personable to say, "Hi, ___ (first name)."

"But you'll want to make some judgment calls as well," says Clay Faircloth (Nashville Career Advancement Center), "for example, if the company is large with a formal culture vs. a small, laid-back start-up. If the person is a VP or above, use Mr. or Ms. when starting an email to them. You want to show the proper respect for those who have achieved a certain professional level of education and/or position." In salutations to women, you can default to Ms. (as opposed to Mrs.) if you're not sure of their marital status.

Hard Copy Communication

Make sure your watermark is turned the correct way when you use stationery for your résumés and cover letters. When holding the paper in front of you with light behind it, the watermark should be right side up and readable. Then, insert the sheets into your printer so that the item prints right side up with the watermark.

It is acceptable to hand-write the recipient's address on an envelope (as opposed to battling your printer to set up for envelope output); just write very neatly. Use a plain or professional return address label—no flowers, puppies, skulls, etc., of course!

Emails

Always include your name in the file name of any attachments you're sending (such as cover letters, résumés, documents containing additional information, etc.). This way, the recipient can quickly identify your information and search for your file more easily. Use this file naming scheme: *Hooper, Jeremy_resume.doc* or *Edwards, Melissa_coverletter.doc*

Backdooring: The Process

Anytime you've just applied for a job, you'll immediately want to "backdoor" your way in as well. That involves emailing a brief note to someone at the company (such as the hiring manager for the position) with your résumé and cover letter attached. Sometimes this is a great bypass of the HR screening process, and other times it's a good double-hit, showing initiative, interest, and thoroughness.

To begin backdooring, check your Networking Log/Target Companies List or at LinkedIn (for any 1st- or 2nd-level connections) when looking for someone to contact. If you still can't find someone, call the company. At LinkedIn, look to see if the person you choose has worked or attended college anywhere you have or whether you're both members of the same association. This can also make a great introduction in the beginning of your email. See the Backdoor Email example in the Appendix for sample wording. Next, use the methods covered in Chapter 4 for obtaining the person's email address. Then, make the email subject line, "Could you help?" Most people like to help—especially when it doesn't take too much time or isn't that difficult.

If you're lucky enough to know someone fairly well at the company at which you just applied, make it easy for them to help you. Think about when you're employed and someone who's in transition asks for your help. Be polite but specific with your request. For example, once I asked Matt, a former coworker, to put in a good word for me with the hiring manager and to forward my résumé and cover letter, since I had just applied online for a job at his company. (I scored a phone interview.)

Then, email your backdoor message with attachments. Sometimes, like with Craigslist, you won't know the company at all. In this case, don't fret about not being able to backdoor. Just use your spreadsheet to keep up with the email address when you apply; then see the section below regarding follow-up.

Backdooring: Legality

During the writing of this book, a reader of my blog mentioned that he'd heard at a presentation that there are now new HR policies that make "backdooring" one's résumé more difficult in order for companies to avoid lawsuits and so that they can pass more aggressive EEOC audits. After checking with several HR professionals, this is what I found: most companies do have a reporting stipulation that requires them to have accurate demographics of those who apply for positions, and HR usually expects applicants to come through them.

But although some companies have more stringent policies regarding what should happen when a manager or employee receives your résumé (as far as turning it over to HR), you should absolutely "backdoor" it after you apply the traditional way. Applying through the "front door" should assuage any concern about fairness or regulations.

If you're a job seeker, apply through the front door, and know that it is still appropriate to do so as well through the backdoor. If you are fortunate enough to get your résumé in front of *the* hiring manager for a position you want—and if you're qualified, the job is actually open, and you made a good impression—it could only be to your benefit to backdoor. If the hiring manager is impressed and wants to hire you, HR is unlikely to hinder the process. If you're on the receiving end of a résumé regarding a position at your company, check to see what your HR department's policy is in this situation.

Following Up

You should *always* follow up on any job for which you've applied, but there's a balance. Doing *too many* follow-ups will annoy HR or the hiring manager; doing *none* will most likely leave you out of the game! So I recommend doing your first follow-up 7 calendar days from the date you applied.

If the person coordinating interviews for the position has not responded, call him or her (see suggested script below), leaving a message if you get voicemail. If in 3 business days, you still have no response, call again. Leave a message if you get voicemail.

> Job Application Call Follow-Up Script: *"Hi, ___, this is ___ (your name). I applied recently for the ___ position. I'm still interested and just wanted to check on the status of that position and what your time frame is for interviewing. My number is ___."*

♛ NOTE--- When leaving any important voicemail, always leave your phone number twice (and spell your name if needed) to make it easier for the person to find your application and call you back.

If you *still* get no response, you can mail a letter (see example in Appendix) about a week after your last follow-up printed on special stationery that you can get at an office supply store—"special" meaning with some unique color or design. This will help it stand out a bit from anything they're getting on plain paper.

If you *are* able to speak to someone when following up and find out the position was filled, ask whether your information can be kept on file in case a similar position comes open. Like with following up on interviews, you could also ask if that person knows of any colleagues or companies that are hiring for similar positions. If you'd like to, make a reminder in your spreadsheet, and call back in about 90 days to politely and subtly see if the person who got the position worked out. (Wink!) Log all notes on progress in your Job Search Log spreadsheet.

RECAP:
- Brush up on how to interact with others at networking events and job fairs.
- Include checking postings on job sites like Indeed and Careerbuilder in your job search strategy. Research any companies or job postings that seem questionable.
- Think about factors such as wages, work environment, and whether you meet at least 75% of the job requirements as you choose which jobs you'll apply for.
- As much as possible, avoid disclosing your specific salary history or requirements.
- Always include cover letters with résumés when applying for jobs; try the T-letter format.
- Unless you are focusing on 1 very specific job, create a few versions of your résumé based on a few types of jobs you're seeking. Customize résumés for certain positions when you feel it's necessary.
- When using résumé paper, print with respect to the watermark.
- For any attachments, name files so they're easily found after they're downloaded.
- Backdoor your résumé and cover letter after applying for jobs the traditional way, and follow up as appropriate.

Other Reading:
- *New Business Networking* by Dave Delaney
- *The Mindset of Networking* by Stewart C. Ross

Endnotes:
1. http://www.jobsearchsmarter.com
2. Right Management, "How To Work A Room," presentation, (January, 2010): 3.
3. https://www.ama.org/career/Pages/Effective-Questions-to-Ask-at-a-Job-Fair.aspx

Woo Hoo!
Interviewing

A few months into one of my recent job searches, I landed an initial phone interview for a marketing position with Asurion. Asurion is one of the major providers of cell phone repair or replacement, back-ending the insurance offered by major providers like Sprint, Verizon, or T-Mobile. One of the first questions the interviewer asked me, with a seemingly doubtful tone, was, "How active is your job search?"

I almost laughed out loud! *"Does she know who she's talking to here?"* I thought. *"Are you kidding me? Does she think most people are lounging around eating bon bons and being a couch potato in between a few calls and online job applications?"* I answered, "Very," and paused for comedic effect before returning to a more professional tone, explaining all I'd been doing over the past few months.

While I know hiring managers and HR professionals run across some slacking job seekers as they're screening candidates, that's definitely not me—or you, I'm sure, since you've taken the time to read this book. Being proactive, networking regularly and strategically, and having the tools you need under your belt will shorten your search and help you appear more valuable and employable as a job seeker.

The first big payoff of your job search efforts is landing interviews with companies you've been targeting, so let's look at how you can not only prepare for but succeed during and after an interview.

CHECK YOURSELF

Here's something to take into account when reaching the interview phase of your search. According to a 2003 survey by the Society for Human Resource Management, these are the top 5 things influencing a hiring manager's decision about each candidate. In order of importance, they are:

1. Interview performance
2. Professionalism in interactions
3. Years of relevant work experience
4. Fit with company culture
5. Appropriate certifications

The top 5 reasons managers didn't offer someone a job (according to a survey by Frank Endicott, former Director of Placement at Northwestern University) should, of course, be avoided—especially if you're a new college grad:

1. Poor personal appearance
2. Being an overbearing know-it-all
3. Lack of planning for career; no purpose of goals
4. Lack of confidence and poise
5. Lack of interest and enthusiasm

PREPARATION

The interview is the fruit of all your searching. (So I guess that makes the fruit of your interviewing landing the job you want!) Congratulations! Your résumé and efforts have accomplished what you wanted: making the phone ring and getting an interview with a company in which you're interested.

When you get that golden call or email and secure an interview, make sure to get the interviewer's name and title, the interview time, date, and address (including any special directions), and ask if there's anything particular you should bring (IDs, references page, portfolio). Some positions, like a graphic designer or craftsman, might be asked to bring along hard-copy samples of their work. Add this information to the top of the Company Information sheet (see sample in Appendix) you'll put together for each interview. Also include the exact title of the position for which you're interviewing.

A quick note about the Company Info sheet: This lists some questions you should ask at the end of your interview. You'll always want to be ready with more than 1 or 2 questions, since some of them may be answered by the interviewer in the course of the conversation. In addition to finding out some things you want to know, having some questions will also help you look prepared and interested. This part of the interview will also allow you an opportunity to show that you've done some research on the company. If the interviewer doesn't ask whether you have any questions and seems to be wrapping up, feel free to jump in respectfully and ask your most important questions.

Research

Author, blogger, career expert, and former exec at Microsoft Dana Manciagli recommends the following: Know the company—and as best you can, about the division and team you'd be a part of. Familiarize yourself with the industry and any lingo or acronyms. Know the job description, and be ready to mirror the important job requirements with SAR examples from your job history.

Research the company's news, awards, and accomplishments. Find out, for instance, who the president is. Familiarize yourself with at least 4 to 5 key facts about the company in case you're asked, "What do you know about us?"

Here are several resources you can use:

- The company's website (obviously!), LinkedIn page, and YouTube channel
- www.glassdoor.com
- www.indeed.com/Best-Places-to-Work
- www.manta.com
- www.referenceusa.com (you'll probably need a library card to access this site)
- www.seekingalpha.com
- www.slideshare.net (a fairly far-fetched resource since you may not find any presentations someone from the company has posted, but why not take a look!)

♛ NOTE--- Apart from Glassdoor's reviews of companies, with most, you'll also find information regarding interview questions users faced as well as reported salary information. With the release of its Facebook application, Glassdoor usage has grown dramatically, and the site continuously attracts new users from around the world. You can also peruse comments from current and former employees at different companies you are considering.

It's always a good idea to check LinkedIn for the photo of the person who will be interviewing you. This way, you can appear more prepared as well as learn more about his or her background. In a networking meeting requested by someone else, when I can tell that person has done their homework on me, I'm impressed! This can happen with interviewers too. Besides potentially impressing them, knowing a few things about your interviewer will also help you personalize the interview, which we'll discuss later.

Questions to Prepare For

While it may seem obvious, review your own résumé before the interview, since the interviewer has already—or will—and may pose questions based on its content. We'll discuss this later in the chapter, but have ready answers for any tough questions you think might be asked about your job history. These could be about things such as why you never finished college, why you were at a job for less than a year, or why you had a long period between certain jobs. Work with your career coach if you need help spinning positive answers.

There are scores of questions you could be asked—anything from accomplishments and your software proficiencies to topics like problem-solving and interpersonal work relations. It's impossible to be ready for every question, and they always seem to ask at least one thing for which you don't have a prepared answer! So instead of stressing or spending too much time in preparation, anticipate the top questions—think about what you'd want to know if you were the interviewer, and come up with those answers. The ones I prepare for are on the Company Information sheet in the Appendix. Let's look at a few:

- **Why should we hire you/what can you do for us?**
  Be prepared to present your qualifications vs. the requirements of the position. Think about what you can do for the company—what you have to offer as it relates to it, the market, and its needs and challenges. Always have at least 4 to 5 concrete reasons why the company should hire you—qualities about yourself and SAR examples to back them up. When relevant, respond with facts and figures, anticipating what you can do in the role for which you're interviewing. For example: "I reduced overtime to near zero and cut turnover by 20% as ___ (job title) at ___ (a former company)," or "I was named 2014 Salesperson of the Year and can bring those same skills to the table in this position."

- **Where do you see yourself in 5 (or 10) years?**
  Obviously avoid any answers like, "Doing your job!" Focus on your skills as they relate to the company and the position. You could say something like, "I see myself drawing on my technical background and managerial skills to advance into an upper management position," or "I want to be the top motion graphics programmer on board."

- **Why did you leave your last position/why do you want to leave your current job?**
  As satisfying as it might be to do so, don't bash or criticize anyone at (or anything about) your current or last company. You could say, "I'm seeking a new position where I can use my skills at a higher level. My current position is limited as far as advancement, so I'd like to have the opportunity to work with ___ (company with which you're interviewing) and handle new challenges, helping the company achieve its goals."[1]

What to Bring

Here's a checklist of what to bring with you to an interview. Descriptions of most have been covered earlier.

- Company Information sheet
- SARs sheet

- Strengths/Questions/Tell Me About Yourself sheet
- Elevator Speech and Exit Statement
- At least 2 copies of your résumé—1 is for your reference and 1 is in case the interviewer asks for it, since frequently, the beautiful formatting you've done has been stripped out of the version HR provided. Have your résumés handy so you don't have to fumble for them. Keeping the other sheets mentioned here in the padfolio (yes, this is apparently a word) is fine; just tuck them out of the way before you're called back for the interview. Note: If you're using a functional résumé, bring a chronological version for yourself as a quick reference or for the interviewer if he or she asks for it.
- Information about your past jobs (start/end dates, salary, addresses, supervisors' names, etc.) This is useful in case you need to fill out an application or submit additional information as a part of the interview. I like to keep a document of this information on Google Drive in order to reduce the amount of papers I bring. Just make sure to update it as you update the file on your computer. Also, paste your references at the top of this document so you'll have those readily available if an application requires it. And remember to bring in your tablet or cell phone so you can access it.
- A professional-looking padfolio/folder (like this one http://bit.ly/padf) to keep all this in, and a pen so you can make notes as needed.

Attire

Before I get into advice on how to dress, know that there will be situations where you may not have to follow standard interview attire. Here are a couple of examples. Although the Scheduling Manager position I had at the record label for which I worked was a dream-come-true foray into the music business, it was a lower-level position. Not wanting to overwhelm the VP who was interviewing me, I dressed in nice slacks and a sweater over a button-down shirt with a tie. (I got the job.)

Another time, in emails where she scheduled our meeting, the owner of an interior design firm talked like it would be more of an initial conversation than a formal interview. I went in my suit and tie but left the coat at home. Use your judgment, since you don't want to go in dressed to the nines and have the interviewer immediately pigeonhole you as overqualified. Beyond these occasional circumstances, it's always good to default to formal clothing when interviewing.

You want to *be* competent and *look* competent. Proper attire for an interview may seem like a no-brainer to most of us, but some people who have sailed through their career on competence lack professional fashion sense, or they've become sloppy. And frequently, an interviewer can be a tough critic. They may want to see if you pay attention to details and how you'll represent the company. In fact, 93% of an interviewer's first impression is formed from a combination of your appearance, the quality of your speech, your confidence, and how you carry yourself within the first few minutes after meeting.[2]

Don't smoke on the way over, since the odor is negative and easily detectable, and don't smoke even if the interviewer offers. Don't use any perfume or cologne; it can either be overpowering, remind an interviewer of bad memories, or in rare cases, cause an allergic reaction. Men and women alike should avoid dressing too fashionably or in a trendy manner. Don't wear glasses with outdated frames or tinting so it doesn't feel like you're hiding or not paying attention. Wearing a watch can show that punctuality is important to you.

Leave in plenty of time to find the office so you can avoid that stress. Arrive about 10-15 minutes ahead of your scheduled interview time so you have time to review your notes, use the restroom, check your appearance, etc. I recommend walking in about 5 minutes before the scheduled interview time. Any earlier, and it may be a nuisance or awkward for you to sit and wait—and you definitely don't want to be late. Come in alone—no kids or friends.[3]

Turn off or silence your cell phone. Few things are more important than this opportunity, and your social stratosphere can wait an hour or so for you to return.

Men should wear a crewneck, not V-neck, undershirt (so it doesn't show through), a dark-colored solid single-breasted suit with a long-sleeved shirt, laundered and pressed. Choose a white or light-colored shirt that complements the color of your suit. Button the jacket when standing. The tip of your tie should end at your belt buckle, and the end of the tie should go through the label in the back to keep it together. Wear a belt that doesn't show signs of wear, with shined clean black shoes and lightweight complementary dark colored socks. The shoes should not look worn out. No more than one ring per hand, with nails clean and trimmed short. Your hair should be trimmed and styled, and be sure to shave (or clean up around your beard, goatee, or moustache if you have one).

Women should wear a dark or neutral suit with a long-sleeved high-necked blouse in white, cream, or a pastel—no dark or wild colors. The skirt should be a conservative hem length and cover your knee when sitting so you project "professional," not "sexy"—and no extreme slits. Shoes should be low- to medium-heeled leather pumps and comfortable—no open-toe or open-back shoes. As far as jewelry, keep it to a minimum: simple (not dangly) earrings, a pin or necklace, ideally no more than one ring per hand, and no more than one bracelet—choose one that doesn't make noise. Makeup should be simple and subtle. Hair color and styling should be appropriate for a professional environment. Nails should be manicured with a light or clear polish. Dark-colored or designer patterned nails may be a distraction. There are different schools of thought (http://bit.ly/intvprs) about bringing a purse in, but in a nutshell, make it a professional looking one that's not too big, and place it on the floor when you sit down to begin the interview.

INTERACTION

Be friendly and respectful to everyone you meet, especially the receptionist. As mentioned in an earlier chapter regarding dropping off résumés, sometimes this person has more influence with hiring managers than you think.[4] Be prepared, confident, positive, and as much as possible, relaxed. If an interviewer has a laid-back style, be personable but stay professional. Besides being qualified and competent, these are the top things an interviewer wants to see in a candidate.[5]

An Encouraging Thought

Interviewing can rattle anyone, from the most experienced exec to a new college grad. But keep this encouraging thought in mind: The interviewer is usually rooting for you. There's already a staffing need that must be resolved, stacks of applicants to evaluate and interview, and the interviewer is most likely handling a portion of the work in the interim. Prepare to knock'em dead, and show that you're the right candidate for the job and the solution to this problem![6]

Upon Meeting

When meeting the interviewer, smile and shake hands firmly. Be prepared to make some small talk (this is where it pays to be up on local events, news, your industry, etc.) in case there's a long walk or an elevator ride to where you'll be interviewed. Wait until he sits first or asks you to have a seat. Keep direct eye contact, and if this is an interview with anyone from a foreign country to which you're considering relocating, abide by any other cultural norms, having researched them ahead of time. Sit up straight to show good posture, and ideally lean toward the interviewer slightly. This posturing can convey attention and interest, which is important since 55% of our communication is nonverbal and affects how we're perceived.[7] Leaning back could convey cockiness.

Communication and Connection

Bear in mind that a big portion of success in an interview is making a connection. A lot of people have experience and knowledge, but in the end, you will most likely be hired on the basis of your character and how strongly the interviewer feels you are the best match for the job.[8]

Keep the mood personable, friendly, and natural but professional. Be sure to smile as you interact. Show enthusiasm for the company and the position, and take time as needed to think about responses to more involved questions.

Whether your interviewer is warm and friendly, a "just the facts" person, or more of a quiet type, it's helpful to try to match his communication style; this can help you make a connection. For example, if he is a quiet, stoic Mr. Spock, and you're a boisterous squirrel, that's likely to rub him the wrong way and deter establishing a very good connection.

You'll be interviewed by people of different ages. As you aim to match communication styles and best relate to each interviewer, keep in mind that each generation views work a little differently and has different values that are most important to them.[9]

As with networking, make sure to listen to what the interviewer is saying so you won't end up asking about something that's already been covered or miss an important piece of information. Despite your enthusiasm, don't finish any of his sentences or interrupt. Try to focus, and don't think about what you want to say next. Take a few notes if needed. And if you have a burning question or statement, write it down so you can continue listening.

If the interviewer's communication style is amiable and you've established some decent rapport, it's good to personalize the interview a bit. While you don't want to dominate the conversation, you do want to get him to talk about himself. Everyone likes to talk about themselves, and I have a friend who swears by (and has been very successful with) this technique. Using the research you did on LinkedIn, you can ask about such things as how he has advanced his career at the company, hobbies, or what brought him to ___ (city). I recommend waiting to do this until you feel the interviewer has asked all his questions.

Your Job History

If there's been a long gap since your last job and the employer asks about it, it's usually because he's hoping to avoid job-hoppers, people that no other company wants to hire (*"there must be a good reason"*), or someone who's been in jail. You can respond with something like this: "Good jobs are hard to find, especially a position like this one at your company. I've interviewed for several jobs, but instead of taking the first opportunity, I'm seeking the right fit with a good company in a position where I can make a solid contribution."[10]

If you're doing independent contract work while you're job hunting and it's relevant to the position for which you're applying, then by all means say something like, "I've kept current in the industry by doing contract work," and then say what that work is. If it's not directly relevant, then focus on transferable skills and how those skills would make you a great candidate for the position.

You also may be asked to explain any challenges in your job history (layoffs, working in very different roles, etc.), so be prepared to defend your situation and the decisions you've made. Play up the positives from those situations by offering specific examples of how you showed proficiencies that would be important to the company.[11] Don't over-explain why you're no longer with your previous employer (or why you're looking to change jobs), but do use your Exit Statement to handle this question if it comes up.

Do's and Don'ts

In my position with the security guard and custodial company I mentioned in Chapter 3, I conducted initial screening interviews with applicants. There were about 4 or 5 questions I always asked in addition to going over certain fields on their applications. One of these was, "What do you feel are your strengths as an employee?" One young woman interviewing for a security job said, "I'm vindictive." Hmm, things not to do!

Don't talk too fast, over-answer questions, or ramble. You can watch the interviewer's body language about the last two! One of my wise former supervisors always encouraged his employees to give just enough information and no more. This way you avoid confusing, overwhelming, boring, or losing the attention of the interviewer. Avoid um's and uh's as much as possible so you can be seen as knowledgeable and prepared. Avoid coming across as conceited, overbearing, negative, or under-confident. Again, steer clear of trashing former employers, supervisors, vendors, coworkers, or universities. If you only want to work in the position for a fairly short time, don't disclose that.

Don't chew gum, and if you have a mint, finish it before you enter the company. Never flirt with or make personal comments about the person interviewing you. And unless he invites you to, avoid calling the interviewer by his first name—no matter his age.

Be sure to have the interviewer cover what specifically he's looking for in the right candidate for the position. From the job description, you should be able to pick out a few key things that would matter most. Anytime you're interviewing (using your judgment), don't be too modest about your accomplishments. You may have been brought up not to be a bragger, but there's a balance, and you need to strike that in order to convey your fit and value.

We'll get into this more in the next chapter, but don't mention salary. Do be prepared to discuss it if the interviewer brings it up. If you're moving through a series of interviews, the company is obviously increasingly interested. Your power increases the longer you can wait to discuss salary, so delay that as long as you can. If pushed for a figure, respond with a reasonable range. You could say something like, "Based on the research I've done, salaries run between $X-Y for this type of position. Is that in line with your salary range?"[12]

If you're prodded about any sensitive subjects —usually also illegal to ask about—such as disabilities, children, or age, just remain calm and professional, be conscious of your body language, and try to discern the interviewer's concern, and answer the question behind the question.[13]

Years ago, an interviewer kept me waiting for about an hour before coming to get me to begin the interview. Luckily I had the time to wait. But if you don't and are running out of time, explain, politely ask to reschedule the interview, and set up a new date and time.[14]

If you're running late for some odd reason, be sure to call ahead to let the interviewer or his or her assistant know that and why. I hope it's a good reason!

OVERQUALIFIED?

Have you ever heard, "We feel you're overqualified for this position"? Talk about feeling like a deflating balloon! How can you salvage an opportunity in this situation?

If you have an interview coming up where you suspect a discussion about being overqualified will arise, prepare ahead of time. In this situation, remember a hiring manager is most likely concerned about:

- Why you're considering the position
- Your leaving if you come across a better job somewhere else
- If they can meet your expectations and how long you'll be happy in this position

So you will need to address these concerns as they surface. In my interview for the job at the security guard and custodial company, the GM straight out asked me, "So how do I know you won't leave and go back to the music industry?" I was honest and explained my situation and career plans and answered his question sincerely, trying to build his confidence that I was not wanting this job as a short-term holdover. (I got the job.) Most interviewers can gauge your sincerity.

Career and interviewing coach Alex Freund advises this strategy: When you get a sense that a hiring manager is labeling you as overqualified, quickly try to discern the root of what he's getting at...concern that the salary for the job is too low, that you'll quit for another job in the near future, etc. Employers don't like turnover. Then, say something like, "I'm sensing you're concerned that money is my main motivator and that I'll take a higher paying position elsewhere as soon as I find one. Is that it?" After the inevitable affirmative response, follow up with, "I do have some rich work experience, but ___ (the company at which you are interviewing) is of particular interest to me because of ___ (your reasons). If I can illustrate that salary is not my primary motivator, would that influence your consideration of me as a candidate?"

Then, round out the discussion with some examples of how things like teamwork, recognition, work environment, the type of work, and/or career advancement are also valuable to you, and mention that money isn't all that's important in the job you're seeking. Being able to talk honestly about a legitimate concern (and potential disadvantage) without getting your feathers ruffled can show your true interest in the position and also build rapport with the interviewer. He may even respect you more, and at the very least, you've cast a positive light on yourself as a viable candidate.[15]

Alternately, your response could be as simple as, "Frequently I seem to be pigeonholed as over-qualified. I feel that being satisfied in a job and having a good fit and a fair salary with room for growth (monetarily and positionally) are more important than whether a position initially seems to completely mirror my education and work history." Feel out the situation, and use your judgment.

PHONE INTERVIEWS

Prepare for phone interviews almost like you would for an in-person interview. Although I've heard dressing up is a good idea, I wouldn't bother unless it makes you feel more confident and professional or unless you're going to be seen on webcam. Call from a quiet room or location. Put your cell phone on vibrate. Know the information fairly well, but feel free to lay out all the sheets you'd normally bring to an interview—this is a big advantage of a phone interview! Speak slowly and loudly enough to be clear.

You'll need a bit of extra time to formulate responses to some behavioral interview questions. So advise the interviewer when you need a moment to think; this way they won't misinterpret the silence. Always clarify the next step before hanging up, and see if you can advocate for an in-person interview. Let the interviewer hang up first.[16] If the interviewer calls you from a number you do not have logged in your Job Search Log spreadsheet, add it from your caller ID or call history. You may need it to reach that person directly when following up.[16]

WRAPPING UP

If you haven't gotten the chance to adequately cover your strengths that are relevant to the position, don't miss the opportunity to emphasize them. I recommend preparing a closing statement.

In the context of the rapport you've established during the interview, and without sounding cocky, try always to conclude by saying something like one of these statements: "I'm confident I can lead the customer service team to increased productivity and use my experience with purchasing and inventory control to boost revenue and reduce returns." "Before we wrap up, it's important that you know___," or "I'd very much like to work for XYZ Company, and if you choose to bring me on board, I won't let you down."

It may feel a little boastful, but this can summarize your skills and abilities, display confidence, help reassure the interviewer that you are the best candidate for the job, and end the interview on a strong, positive note. After all, if you were the hiring manager and choosing from your top few picks, wouldn't you be more likely to lean toward the candidate who made it clear she wants the job?

Make sure you know what the next step is in the interviewing or hiring process. Be sure to get a business card at the end of the interview, since sometimes you won't have, for instance, the interviewer's email address or direct phone number. Smile, say thank you, and firmly shake hands before you leave.

AFTERWARDS

Evaluation

An interview is not only for the employer to evaluate you but an opportunity for you to learn more about the job, the company, its culture, your supervisor, the salary, etc. After the interview, you will obviously have a better idea of these things and can decide whether this position is for you. Here's a rare example from my own experience. After I had an interview scheduled, but before I went in for the appointment, I found out from two colleagues that the owner (who interacts with the position for which I was interviewing) was a jerk. Knowing that and enough other inside information, I decided that this company was not a good fit for me.

The interview went alright, but afterwards, having made my decision, I simply did not send a thank-you letter or follow up. I hoped they would not call me for a second interview, since one of the two colleagues I mentioned earlier still worked there—and got me the interview. Luckily, the company did not follow up, so I was off the hook and able to avoid any awkwardness.

So if your impression of the company is positive and it's a job in which you are still interested, don't get hung up on the salary. Take a holistic view when making your decision. Consider company culture, scope of responsibility, fit with your personality and career path, opportunities for growth and advancement, number of supervisors, and work/life balance. You want to be happy with—and successful in—your new job, since you'll probably want to work there for several years. And as for salary, sometimes if it isn't much more than you had (or have at your current job), you might consider taking the position anyway since you may be burned out, ready for a change, or know that a lateral move may open more doors in the long term.[17]

Follow Up

What you do after the interview is just as important as *how you did* in the interview. Send a thank-you letter a day or two after the interview. (There's a sample in the Appendix.) You can use it as an opportunity to sell yourself a bit more or address anything you feel didn't go well— or that you forgot to mention in the interview. Then note the name of the interviewer, date of the interview, date you sent the thank-you letter, and a date to follow up in your Job Search Log.

Follow up with a phone call in around 8 calendar days or a few days after the interviewer said he'd reach a decision on who would get the offer. During this call, you want to convey your continued interest in the position, ask how the hiring process is going, or answer any questions the interviewer might have (or any new ones you have.) Don't ask how you did in the interview, whether you're being considered for the job, or about salary or benefits.[18]

Turndowns

Like listening to a wishy-washy weather forecast while driving through rain, there's a 100% chance that you will be turned down for some jobs for which you interview. Treat that experience as an opportunity. You can do several things:

- You should always reply to the rejection email you receive, or send a letter asking the interviewer to please keep you in mind should a similar position come open.
- It's kind of a gutsy move, but if you like, you can call and ask the interviewer about specifics—things you could have done differently or answered better in the interview or why your skills were not a match for the job. Then, incorporate any feedback you feel appropriate into your interviewing style going forward.
- Ask if the hiring manager knows of any other companies or colleagues hiring for a similar position.
- If it's a situation where the job for which you interviewed opens up on a regular basis, ask if you can call every 4 to 6 weeks to inquire about new openings.[19]
- About 3 months after the new person (who got the job you wanted) begins, call or email the interviewer to gently touch base with a reminder of your availability. Sometimes the person that was hired doesn't make it past the standard 90-day evaluation period.

Whether your response is a letter or email, always make sure to include your email address and phone number so the interviewer has a quick, easy way to respond.

SECOND INTERVIEWS

Frequently, a second interview is required. For the most part, prepare for a second interview like you did for the first. Men, if you only have one suit, dress in a blazer, with complementary-colored slacks and a button-down shirt with a tie for the second interview. Ladies, wear a different but professional formal outfit.

Try to find out whether this will be a panel, group (meaning you're one of several people all being interviewed together), one-on-one, or circuit of interviews. Do the research ahead of time in preparation to answer questions about what salary you would accept. Review your notes about the company and any notes you took during the first interview that you feel are relevant. Bring the same sheets you did for the first interview, and get answers to the Second Interview questions listed on the Strengths, Questions, Tell Me About Yourself sheet and any others important to you.

Ask about the timeline of the hiring process, and know what the next step is for you. Take note as best you can of the names of all the additional people interviewing you, and send them thank-you notes the next day. If some of them are based in a different office, call to get their mailing addresses.

RECAP:

- Prepare for your interview by researching the company and your interviewer(s.)
- Review your résumé, and use the Company Information sheet to prepare for the main questions you may be asked.
- If applicable, be ready to handle being labeled overqualified or discuss any challenges in your job history.
- Assemble and bring to the interview the items on the What to Bring Checklist in this chapter.
- Dress accordingly for the position for which you're interviewing.
- Be on time, and if you need to reschedule due to excessive wait time, do so.
- Interact effectively, building rapport and making a connection with the interviewer.
- Reassure the interviewer with a confident closing statement, and get a business card.
- Follow up on the company's decision.
- Decide how you wish to handle being turned down.

Endnotes:

1. Nashville Career Advancement Center, "The Most Common Tough Questions Job Interviewers Ask and How to Answer Them," *Helpful Hints for the Mature Job Seeker Participant Guide*: 9-10.
2. https://www.themuse.com/advice/the-little-interview-mistakesthat-cost-you-big-time
3. *Nashville Career Fairs Directory and Career Guide* (July, 2010): 71-72.
4. Frieda James Personnel "Interview Tips": 1.
5. *Nashville Career Fairs Directory and Career Guide* (July, 2010): 72.
6. Mark Marshall, Lee Hecht Harrison, "Two Things To Remember That Will Put You At An Advantage," *handout* (January, 1999).
7. http://www.forbes.com/sites/keldjensen/2012/06/12/the-naked-truth-how-body-language-reveals-the-real-you
8. Rodney Laughlin, *Getting the Job: A Guide For Employment Seekers* (1987): 25.
9. Right Management, "Interviewing Strategies," presentation (January, 2010): 9-10.
10. Nashville Career Advancement Center, "The Most Common Tough Questions Job Interviewers Ask and How to Answer Them," *Helpful Hints for the Mature Job Seeker Participant Guide*: 10.
11. *Nashville Career Fairs Directory and Career Guide* (July, 2010): 76.
12. Right Management, "Interviewing Strategies," presentation (January, 2010): 5.
13. Right Management, "Interviewing Strategies," presentation (January, 2010): 7.
14. Frieda James Personnel "Interview Tips": 1.
15. http://www.personalbrandingblog.com/perceived-as-overqualified-what-now and Nashville Career Advancement Center, "The Most Common Tough Questions Job Interviewers Ask and How to Answer Them," *Helpful Hints for the Mature Job Seeker Participant Guide*: 10.
16. Right Management, "Interviewing Strategies," presentation (January, 2010): 4.
17. Karla Ahern and Naomi Keller, "Salary Negotiations in the New Year," *Marketing News*, (February 2014): 71.
18. Right Management, "Interviewing Strategies," presentation (January, 2010): 11.
19. Rodney Laughlin, *Getting the Job: A Guide For Employment Seekers* (1987): 33.

7

Hashin' it Out
Negotiating and Accepting a Position

THE DANCE: A FAIR BALANCE

Ah, money. I think hiring managers and interviewees alike both dread this part of the process. Years ago, one of my former supervisors offered up a great observation about the importance of the employer and the candidate striking a fair balance when it comes to compensation: If the company lowballs the salary and the candidate accepts, she may quit as soon as she runs across a higher paying job. That will ultimately cost the company even more, since many businesses invest significant time and cost in recruiting and assimilating new employees. On the other hand, if the candidate asks for an unfairly high salary and the company grants it, the company may be breathing down her neck, pushing to get the value they're paying for since such a high figure was settled on—and possibly even targeting her in the next round of layoffs. But when you feel like your compensation is worth the responsibilities you're about to assume and the value you bring to the company, and the company gets a satisfied, qualified employee without overpaying, it's a win-win.[1]

THE REASONS: WHY SHOULD YOU NEGOTIATE?

Most employers expect to negotiate during the hiring process and almost always are prepared to go higher than the initial offer. Once you're in the role and working, they may even respect you more because you had the *cojones* to bring up the issue and make a convincing case. In most situations, it never hurts to see if you can inch up the compensation, since you might get into the job and discover it's more responsibility and work than you anticipated—or the employer conveyed! Another thought to consider is that if you bite on the first figure thrown out, it may take you years in cost-of-living increases or standard raises to get to the level you might have achieved negotiating on the front end.

You have the most bargaining power after the employer has decided on you but before you've accepted the offer. (Ooo, what a head rush; don't get cocky!) Once you've accepted, the ball's in the company's court, and you may experience seasons where all increases are frozen. This happened to me.

At one large company where I worked, I jumped through all the hoops, completing presentation requirements, time-consuming training, and every other expectation my department had of me—sometimes even staying late off the clock to manage my workload. Come the first evaluation period, due to the economy, the company granted *no one* a raise. Toward the end of the next year, I had again busted my hump to do exemplary work with fingers crossed for a raise. Instead, I was laid off in a department downsizing a couple of months before evaluation time. Foiled twice!

♛ NOTE--- Keep in mind, union constraints may limit flexibility on salary levels, no matter how many university degrees you have.

THE PREPARATION: BE A DETECTIVE

If you are truly interested in a job and feel an offer is forthcoming, do your homework. Thoroughly consider the company in order to decide whether it's a good fit for you. Discuss it with your spouse, friends, or family. Research the advancement potential and a fair salary for your location and job title.

Author Dan Miller says the *responsibilities* of the job determine the salary, not your experience, education, or previous salary.[2] So keep this in mind as you formulate how to make your case for the salary you want.

In most cases, you'll know when you're getting close to an offer, so it's important to be ready for that inevitable and vital conversation. Don't expect a huge pay jump or to be at the top of the range for the position, especially if you're between jobs. Be realistic, and keep in mind that at some large companies, there may not be much flexibility in the salaries since they may be stringently defined.

First, you'll want to use an online salary calculator to determine a monetary range that you're willing to accept—a rough idea of what you're worth and what a fair salary is for the position. (Where were we without the internet?!) My favorite site is www.payscale.com, which is very in-depth, but here are several others:

- www.careeronestop.org/SalariesBenefits/Sal_default.aspx
- www.glassdoor.com
- www.jobstar.org/tools/salary/index.htm
- http://salary.careerbuilder.com
- www.salary.com

♛ NOTE--- The figures at www.salary.com and similar sites represent a range of what people in that job are getting paid across many companies. The lowest figure in the range is not necessarily the best starting salary for that job.

Second, when starting to negotiate, have a story as to *why* you deserve what you're asking for. And no matter how close you are to being the top candidate, you'll get further by *asking* rather than *demanding*. You'll have to anticipate your duties in the position and convey the value you'll add to the company and the role. This should come easily if you've prepared thoroughly for the interview and researched the salary range.[3] We'll explore more about what to say later in this chapter.

THE OPTIMAL TIME: STALL...FOR LOVE!

As stated earlier in the book, it's still good practice to delay any discussion of salary as long as possible. Again, you have the most bargaining power during that window of time after the employer has decided you're the best person for the job but before you've accepted the offer. Let the employer fall in love with you first before laying out salary and benefit expectations. Traditional wisdom holds that you should never talk salary before the offer. Once you *get* the offer, you can always negotiate for more of what you'd like.[4]

However, know that some employers may ask you how much you're expecting even as early as the initial phone screening, just to make sure you're both in the same ballpark. So if they don't mention a salary figure but press you for yours, as we covered in the interviewing chapter, first try saying something like, "Let's talk a little more about the position to see if there's a match." Then, if they still insist, answer with a range, making it clear that it's up for discussion.[5]

THE MATCH: CONSIDERATION OF THE OFFER

Take into account all that you know about the company from your targeted networking, company research, and everything covered in the interview. Weigh it out before making a decision—ideally *ahead* of the job offer. Consider the following about any position you're thinking about accepting:[6]

- How well the position fits into the career path you're forging
- Security/stability of the position and industry
- Work environment - office or cube, view, noise level

- Lifestyle fit - length of commute, hours, flexibility, travel involved
- Compensation - pay, bonus structure, benefits, 401k, stock options
- Company car or cell phone
- Recognition and the opportunity for promotion/advancement (if you've had a chance to get a sense of these things)
- The management style of the company

Once you've negotiated the best salary possible with the company, if you still feel like you deserve more, consider asking for non-salary perks: more paid vacation time, an early performance review at the 90-day or 6-month point in efforts toward a raise, relocation or tuition assistance, sign-on or future bonus, flex time; telecommuting, or stock options.

Don't forget that the job title can be negotiable, too! For instance, I interviewed for a Customer Service Rep position. But for the experience and skills I was bringing to the table—not to mention the below-range compensation I was offered—I felt some negotiation was in order, so I brought up title. Reassuring the owner that it was not so I could use that as coercement later or for any other ulterior reason, I gave my reasons and politely asked if my title could instead be Customer Service Manager. He agreed, and I got the job.

After all, some of the things you can bring into play won't cost your employer much—or in some cases anything at all! And that job title will forever look far better on my résumé as "manager" vs. "rep." You can use www.salary.com to check various wordings of job titles in your field.

THE ANSWER: ACCEPTING A JOB OFFER—2 WAYS YOU CAN GO

There are 2 main ways you can respond to a job offer. Which you choose will depend on whether you want to negotiate.

If I sense an impending offer on a job I want and have been interviewing for, I like to keep the scripts shown in italics below in my wallet, since I never know when "the call" will come. Response Option 1 deals with a situation where you'd like to negotiate or need to discuss something—there may be a health, family, or childcare situation that you don't feel comfortable breezing over on the phone. These types of important conversations should be held in person if possible. (Option 2 is for a "jump on it now" or fair compensation acceptance situation. Print both on the back of the elevator speech you keep in your wallet or purse for quick reference.) Here's a sample response:

1. *"That's great! This is the culmination of my efforts to take the best next step in my career. I'm sure I'm the right person for this position. Could we set up a time to meet, wrap up the details, and discuss a few last questions?"*

Then, ideally, the hiring manager can schedule a time when you can meet again to address any additional issues or concerns and move forward. Furthermore, this gives you more time to think through the position even more and talk with your friends or family.

I must play devil's advocate here and bring up one concern: While it's rare for an offer to be retracted, you never know when a prospective employer is going to expect a same-conversation acceptance or interpret an Option 1 approach as weak interest on your part. If you've done the research we discussed earlier and already made up your mind that you want to work there, typically you should be able to make a decision quickly. Sometimes you may lose the top-candidate spot if you ask for too much time. This happened to me once: When the hiring manager called to offer me that first (dream) job at the record label I mentioned earlier in the book, I asked if I could come in and talk more (about second-interview type questions to see if I could nudge the salary up, etc.).

Because of this, I almost lost the position. Although he agreed to the meeting, he took my response as lack of interest and told me that in the meantime he was going to contact a few other previous interviewees about their current interest. I ended up getting the job, but that was a close call and a big lesson learned. So use your judgment, and be ready to jump on a position if you sense the door may close quickly or if you feel like everything offered *is* fair (which we'll cover in Option 2).

Come to the meeting you requested well prepared to negotiate. Brush up on the things discussed earlier in this chapter: why you're worth it, what you want to say, a salary range, and any other points you want to cover or negotiate. Be professional and respectful. It won't be comfortable or easy, but it will definitely be worth the effort if you feel you deserve more than what's being offered.

Longtime New York career coach and author Ellis Chase advises this: Stay in the mindset that you're still in an interview. For your first couple of questions, ask easy things like when the 401k match will start or about reporting relationships. The third question should address your top priority. When nudging up salary, you'll need to sell yourself again, reminding the hiring manager of your experience, education, and why you're worth more. The fourth question should be another easy topic that could be followed by another tough one.[7]

When getting down to the numbers as you negotiate salary, see if you can get the hiring manager to play his hand first, saying something like, "I've done some research as far as salary for this type of position. What were you thinking?" In a recent meeting I had, a wise hiring manager smiled and said, "You go first." If this happens, you have to play ball, so you could respond with "Based on the research I've done, salaries for similar positions run between $X and $Y. Would $Z work with your budget?"

Your Z figure needs to be on the high end of the range you found since this will be the first hard number thrown out and will likely be reduced as you negotiate—a company's first offer is probably not their top figure. You'll want to have your rock bottom figure in mind—an amount you *must* have to accept the job. The hiring manager's response will either be acceptable or a bit too low. If it's the latter, like Ellis Chase advises, you'll want to re-sell yourself. Here's a sample:

"You need a reliable, experienced business development manager you can trust who's a creative make-it-happen guy. With me, you're getting that in addition to my large local and international network and resources, as well as my design and writing abilities." Then close with, "With my success in timely project delivery and first-rate customer service, if you could see fit to start at $A, I can assure you you'll be very happy, and this will be a solid step in the right direction toward ___." (Fill in what you feel like the company needs most in this position, e.g., "taking your business development efforts to the next level and establishing sales in Canada and Mexico within my first 6 months.") If you're really interested in the job and the manager will not budge on the salary, you could start to discuss other compensation items covered earlier in this chapter that are important to you.

Again, if you feel the compensation being offered *is* fair (or if you're done with Option 1 and ready to accept the job) you can respond with something like this:

> 2. *"Great! I accept. This evening I'd like to email you my understanding of everything we've discussed, and if you could reply with a letter of hire, then I can look at my calendar (or speak with/give notice to my current employer) and let you know the first date I can begin. And just to let you know, ___."* (This is where you can mention any prior obligations such as your monthly commitment to a professional association, a series of doctor appointments, or a trip you already have planned.)

Whether you're going into a meeting or anticipate negotiation by phone, I encourage you to personalize the samples covered in this section and script out what you need for your situation; then practice. Definitely take notes anytime you negotiate, and verbally summarize and identify the next step before you leave or hang up.

THE DOCUMENTATION: THE LETTER OF HIRE

If you're currently working, you definitely want to have the letter of hire/offer letter before giving notice, since you don't want to quit your current job before you have something in writing from your new employer. Your email should detail title, salary, benefits, travel expectations, and any other important information that's been discussed. There's a sample Letter of Hire Request/Summary Email in the Appendix. Your email will also serve as a gentle reminder for the hiring manager to cover these points in your letter of hire. Upon receipt, review this letter closely to make sure it contains everything you understood and expected and that nothing important is omitted or looks out of line.

Frequently, employers are in a hurry to get you started working. Withholding your start date until you have their letter of hire is good leverage—and a motivator. Here's an example: Had I not used this approach in one of my recent positions, I'm sure I would have started work and never gotten a letter of hire, having only a few discussions to go on.

That situation is asking for trouble down the road if nothing is in writing, since either party could forget or have misunderstood something. Going off a verbal agreement won't get you very far when job duties, pay rate, raise structure, etc., are being discussed from memory later on.

Having a letter of hire can also come in handy if you're laid off. For example, while in the negotiations phase with one of my former employers, I learned that they wanted to pay the commission part of my compensation annually. Long story short, this was not acceptable to me, so I pushed back until the hiring manager agreed to make it quarterly.

Three months into the job (and at the end of Q2), I had yet to receive my first commission (since I had accomplished what it was based upon). Shortly after that point, the company cut about 10 positions—including mine—and because I could prove my commission structure to HR with my letter of hire, the owner made good on the pending commission and had HR pay it along with my final check and severance pay. Cover your butt!

RECAP:
- A company's first figure is usually not the only option, so always negotiate, or at least do the research to see what's fair for the position.
- Research fair compensation *before* the offer comes, and script out why you're worth what you're asking for.
- Remember, there are other things besides money for which you can negotiate.
- Wait as long as you can to bring up salary, until the employer is feeling they must have you.
- Consider the job itself in addition to the salary and benefits before giving the company your decision.
- If you want to negotiate, if at all possible, do so in person. If you've done the homework, and the offer is fair, you can accept without pushing for more.
- After accepting a new job, always get a letter of hire—especially before giving notice to your current employer.

Other Reading:
- *Salary Tudor* by Jim Hopkinson

Endnotes:
1. Daniel Paulk, "Recognize Your Right to Negotiate Salary," *Job News, Nashville Edition* (Feb., 2000): 31.
2. Dan Miller, *48 Days to the Work You Love* (2005): 141.

3. Karla Ahern and Naomi Keller, "Salary Negotiations in the New Year," *Marketing News*, February (2014): 71.

4. http://www.bizjournals.com/nashville/morning_call/2014/06/whens-the-right-time-to-talk-about-salary-during-a.html

5. http://www.isothefunforeverjob.com/blog/should-you-bring-up-salary-in-a-job-inter-view-forbes

6. Rick Ross, "Salesmanship in the Job Search," *Nashville Career Transition Group hand-out* (May, 2007).

7. http://www.isothefunforeverjob.com/blog/how-to-negotiate-your-salary-once-you-have-the-job-offer-forbes

8

It's My First Day
After You Have the Job

Some of the sweetest times in your life are those spaces between when you land your new position and the first day you begin. Before you skip off to the movies or plop down with bonbons to veg in front of the TV, use this time to get a few things in order and make the transition into your new job less stressful. Several will be discussed in more depth.

ACTION ITEMS

Before the First Day
- If you have certain things from home (photos, office supplies, notes) you like to have at the office, box those up and have them ready to bring with you on day 1 so you can set them up during your lunch break.
- If you have children, plan with your spouse who will do what based on the hours/days of your new position.
- Follow any instructions your employer has given you, and return any forms they've asked you to complete. Some will require drug screenings and background checks.

During the First 3 Months
- Treat yourself! You've worked hard for months. Buy something from your wish list.
- Alert your state labor department of your new job and start date so you can arrange for your unemployment benefits to stop the day before your first day of work. Or do whatever your state requires. With some, you simply stop filing, and your case will automatically close after a certain amount of time.
- Turn off job posting alerts (and de-activate your résumé) at sites like Indeed, Careerbuilder, and Beyond and at any job boards on professional association sites. Change preferences as

needed regarding communications from LinkedIn, but hold off on updating your LinkedIn profile at this point.

• Set email filters to direct messages from job posting groups (such as CABLE or career transition groups) to your email account's trash folder.

• Delete all recurring job search related events on your calendar. I recommend logging the wording of the longer calendar items in your Action Plan before doing so since you will need them during your next job search.

• Alert your headhunters that you have landed and to change your status to inactive (but not to delete you from their system). Thank them for their help.

• When possible, roll your 401k, etc., into your new company's retirement offering.

• Add information about your new job onto your Older Jobs and Additional Info document.

• Early on, ask about your new company's file back-up policy/procedure. You may need to establish a more manual routine to regularly and thoroughly back up your important work files if the company's system doesn't do it automatically.

• Give your new work phone number to your spouse, children (and/or their schools, caretakers, etc.), and parents. Add your supervisor's contact information into your phone.

• Compile a list of job duties or questions about the company that you're not certain about and meet with your supervisor for clarification..

• Find out how to set up direct deposit. Make sure you understand your vacation time and benefits. At the proper time, set up things like insurance and employee retirement funds. If desired, cancel any independent insurance policies you have so they end before your coverage through your new employer begins.

• Make a new budget after receiving your first paycheck.

• Save up a cushion fund. Start by getting $1,000 squirreled away, and don't dip into it. Then shoot for enough savings to cover 3-6 months of living expenses as a full-fledged back-up fund.[1] You could set up a monthly automatic transfer from your checking account to your savings.

• Meet as many coworkers as you can early on. Not only is this beneficial in case you have questions about something, but it helps build goodwill and speeds up the process of fitting into the family and culture of the company. Pay attention to the hierarchy —both official and unofficial—as you go.

• Volunteer for things as you see opportunities arise. Once I was asked to judge a potluck dessert contest—boy, was someone dead on with that one!

Typically, you're in like Flynn (whoever he was!) as soon as you make it past the 90-day mark. By this point, you've gotten a feel for the job, the company culture, and the customer base, and your supervisor has a more thorough impression of you now. So if you're happy and planning to stay on with the company, proceed with this last section:

After the 90-Day Mark

• Schedule any doctor or dentist appointments you may have been putting off for after your insurance coverage is active.

• Email your networking colleagues to thank them for their help and to let them know where you've landed and what your new position is. Facebook message or email your friends and family to do the same. (I like to wait until after the 90-day mark since at this point I know I'm going to stay, and the company plans to keep me on. Obviously I may mention it earlier to close colleagues and friends.)

- Cross-train someone, or at least make sure someone can handle your top duties when you go on vacation or are out sick. Work with your supervisor to figure out the best plan of action.
- Clean up your email "job" folder. A good rule of thumb is to delete messages 9 months or older.
- Add the new job to your LinkedIn profile, and update your headline (and—if relevant—your city and industry). Delete the "Seeking" part of the information in the Summary section of your profile. Remember, when in Edit mode, set the "Notify Your Network" option at the upper right of the screen to Yes or No depending on if you'd like to announce your new position with a LinkedIn email update.
- Update your online profile at any professional organization where you're a member.
- Don't throw all your networking out the window. Try to attend at least one networking event a month. I'll go into more depth on this later in this chapter.

Contact Info

Remember my dream-come-true job at the first record label? Well, on my third day, I was sick as a dog. I hate missing work—especially that soon at a new job. A few thoughts went through my mind: *"Will my boss and coworkers assume I am a slacker? Will they think I am going to quit?"* But I was so sneezey and contagious it would have been a mess to come in and make others sick. All this to say, you never know when you're going to be out sick or have a situation that requires you to be out of the office.

So put your supervisor's email address, office, and (if appropriate) cell phone numbers into your phone's contact list. This way, if you need to call out sick, are running late, or have something urgent come up, you won't have the added stress of hunting down this information last minute. This is all part of being dependable and reliable and lets your supervisor know your job is important to you and that you respect him or her as well as your coworkers.

Expectations and Clarification

Remember the *Seinfeld* episode in which George debated whether to follow his boss into the men's room when they were discussing a project? He didn't. The boss went straight to a stall, closed the door, thought George had followed him in, and kept talking. George missed a lot of detail about a project he was supposed to do. Unless your supervisor has already covered them, establish or clarify measurable goals and the expectations of your department or supervisor. This way, even before your first evaluation, you can have a way to make sure you're on track and know what you're aiming for or need to achieve. Asking about a 30-60-90 day plan would be a good way to start this conversation. Get clarification on things you're not sure of; this will save you time and possible embarrassment.[2]

The Green

As you may recall, unemployment pay takes several weeks to begin, so now—while you have a job—save up at least $1,000 or 4 weeks of pay in case you are laid off for some reason.

This will give you a cushion to make it through that initial waiting period for benefits to start. Furthermore, begin debt reduction at this point if your new salary is larger than your previous one. My blog (www.kurtkirton.com) has some great information on money management and budgeting. Search for the Moolah Mondays series.

Networking

It's always good—albeit typically challenging—to maintain and grow your network after you land a new job. Whether it's attending 1 mixer a month, using LinkedIn to keep up and interact with your network, or forwarding a pertinent tip, article, or event announcement to one of your colleagues, do your best to maintain interaction with as many folks as you can. You'll really want to draw on your network in times of career transition, and if your new job is in something like sales, you'll obviously want to contact people in your network.

Attend 1 or 2 of your favorite networking events per month. As you find information that could be helpful to someone in your network, send it to them with a short personal message about what's going on with you professionally or personally. Ask about what's new with them, how their work is going, or what major projects they're working on. Join or keep up your membership and attendance with a professional organization in your field.

Other reasons you should continue to attend some networking events are:[3]

- Making more connections and growing your network
- Learning about a topic of interest to you or important to your field
- Meeting experts on topics that interest you
- Sharing your knowledge. Who knows—maybe *you* should be presenting!
- Meeting others who may be interested in your company's products or services

ADVANCING YOUR CAREER AND MAKING YOURSELF INDISPENSIBLE

Your supervisor and new coworkers will be watching and evaluating you—making up their mind about what kind of person and coworker you are and what they can expect from you. Let's look at what should you be doing to integrate yourself into the company, move up the ladder, and establish yourself as a less likely target come staff-reduction time.

Dress the Part

Appearance continues to be important beyond the interview. It can help you succeed in your new position and even make people feel more comfortable with you. Beyond dressing appropriately, on your first day, notice how your same-sex coworkers dress—or even the attire of your supervisor or those you want to emulate. If your boss leans more conservative, think in that direction.

Solve 'em, Don't Be One

Cultivate a "fix it before it breaks" mindset. After a few months, as you encounter problems or see them in your company, show initiative, and brainstorm a solution or 2 instead of complaining or avoiding them. Then, present this information to your manager or the appropriate point person. Heading off a potential problem before a trickle becomes a flood will save not only money but "face" and time for your department and/or the company. Problems create an opportunity to show your value to the company and contribute to growth.

And speaking of problems, all employees will encounter them at some point or another. So regardless of whether your boss has an open-door policy, avoid the big-kid mentality. Many people come to work expecting everything to go smoothly and to have someone else fix any problems. While it might be a relief to offload problems onto somebody else, it will convey that you're not ready for more responsibility and don't want to be a person that can get things taken care of.[4]

Panic—the Topic (not an Action Item)

Frequently, when you're the new kid on the block, you'll feel overwhelmed. In addition to training, you'll probably need to flesh out your own system of backing up important files, get a grip on corporate culture, and figure out how you'll handle email and customer requests, in addition to coping with new employee computer issues and learning how to best manage your workload. At this stage, there's a lot on your plate, which can stress you out if you let it. Realize that most people will be patient; they know you're new and still learning. Resist any temptation to freak out or panic. And if a situation arises or a project fails, keep a cool head, and approach the situation as a challenge, not a disaster. Brainstorm ways to address and resolve the situation.

Positivity and Stress Management

Again, as with the beginning of the job search process, perception is reality. Whether you're meeting coworkers on the phone, being introduced personally, or bumping into them before meetings, just smile, be friendly, and come off like you have everything under control—even if you feel like you don't!

Project an air of confidence and competence, and keep in mind the hiring manager chose *you* for this job because he or she has faith that you'll do the job well. And if you must vent, do it to friends, family, your Stephen minister, pet, or to yourself quietly with your office door shut or outside the building. It's okay to take breaks and go outside if you're feeling run over or stressed out.

Watch Your Mouth

Refrain from gossip, and don't vent to new coworkers who may be training you even if they've said you're welcome to call on them when you're stressed or freaking out. Usually, these people have more loyalty to your mutual supervisor and may be asked how you're doing—or disclose what you've said in confidence for any number of ulterior reasons. Even in happy hour settings or during off-site events, don't air your complaints to work friends. This can come back to bite you since often word gets around about who said what.[5]

And watch your tone: even neutral comments can come off negatively if delivered with a nasty tone.[6] Once, when I was a temp hoping to be hired on, the company at which I was assigned had a retreat. Employees and temps alike were bussed out to a campground full of cabins for fellowship and fun and to discuss work and brainstorm ideas. In one breakout session, the leader told everyone, "We're open to all ideas and thoughts. Don't hold back. This is an open discussion!" So being the productive employee and forward thinker that I am, toward the beginning of the meeting in the enthusiasm of being included, I asked how the ideas we were generating and capturing would be processed after the retreat was over so that nothing would be forgotten or neglected later.

I think this was taken negatively—possibly since I was a temp—and the company terminated my services a couple of days after the retreat, citing "fit" and a few other weak examples of why they weren't happy with me. All that to say, if you're the new guy, watch *how* you say things as much as *what* you're saying. You're still in the process of establishing a reputation and fitting in with the organization. You want to avoid coming off as abrasive or critical too early on, and you don't want to be seen as the new guy who wants to revamp everything without knowing much yet about the company. But when appropriate, and in time (depending on the urgency of the issue), do speak up on important things you see that need addressing.[7]

Creativity

When working on projects that require creativity, learn how to "uni-task." Focus on just one thing, and block out everything else as you brainstorm. If need be, forsake your office for a place that's calm, inspiring, or conducive to creative thought. Capture ideas as you have them; make a note or keep a list, since the mind is good at producing ideas but not so great at storing or recalling them. Creativity is the result of preparation, discipline, and routine.[8]

Staying Current

Continue to stay up on developments and news in your industry—trends, changes, and breakthroughs. (Actually, continue this practice from your job search!) This knowledge can help you be a forward thinker and create new opportunities for your company or customers while putting yourself, your career, and your organization at an advantage. Staying in the know can also position you to help your company better maneuver any choppy waters you foresee or encounter.[9] And always be learning at work. Be open to picking up new skills. It'll be time well spent, even if it means you stay a little late on a Friday to finish up your typical duties or a project that you didn't have time to work on earlier that day.[10]

Dealing With Change

When I think about how most of us are averse to change, I recall a scene in a *Family Guy* episode in which Peter has carved off part of the house—Stewie's room—to use for one of his hare-brained projects. Stressed and irritated upon entering the room and finding a huge opening to all outdoors, Stewie yelps, "I don't like change!" As much as we all know change is inevitable, do your best to be adaptable and handle change with grace. Highly promotable employees are willing to adapt and roll with the punches; that's what every company needs—especially companies nurturing growth.[11]

Culture

I can't imagine any company that wouldn't expect its new hires to fit in. Pay attention to your coworkers and your new employer's culture so you can adapt and mesh with it. Don't be too jokey for the first several months as you're fitting in and getting to know people. Use your judgment, but try to withhold your opinions, and limit giving much input. Wait to criticize or suggest much unless you need to establish procedure that will be foundational to your job. Don't play politics until you're sure of the players and those who hold the power (officially and unofficially). Avoid touchy subjects like race, religion, sex, and salary. Keep your tone "discuss," not "argue."[12] Before the 90-day mark—or at any point early on—you don't want to get the old, "It's not a good fit for you here. We're letting you go."

People Skills

Fitting in and building respect and a good reputation are crucial early on. One of my former supervisors used to flowchart out the positions and divisions in each company he worked for soon after he began. This initiative can aid your understanding of the company and who you could approach if you have an issue or need beyond the scope of your department. If you're just not sure how to track this information down, your supervisor may have done this flowcharting already or be able to help you with the process.[13]

Have a brief "elevator speech" for what you do in your position. You can use this as you meet your fellow employees.[14] Starting in your area, meet as many people as you can, even if they're outside your department or not on your floor. This will help you develop good relationships with coworkers and build goodwill.[15]

Cultivate a network of relationships with coworkers at many levels. Higher-ups can help give you perspective from a management point of view; those at your level can answer questions and help you become more effective in your work. Avoid the complainers and negative Nellies.[16]

Communicate clearly with vendors and coworkers alike, and really listen as you train and take in things about your duties and the company.[17, 18]

Show energy, enthusiasm, and excellence in your work, and strive to be visible. Find little ways to subtly toot your horn. Most supervisors are pretty overwhelmed, and it doesn't hurt to work what you've recently accomplished into a conversation. Think about things like great customer feedback, compliments on your work from coworkers and higher-ups, meeting deadlines ahead of schedule, and positive facts or figures like sales achievements or how much you just saved the company.

Making valuable contributions to projects can showcase you as a standout collaborator. Big projects need collaborative teams to carry them out. Perfect your persuasion skills, and if you're not really a detail person, cultivate an eye for detail. Identify the positives and benefits of the thing in question; solicit feedback from friends, colleagues, and coworkers; then match the communication style of those you need to persuade when presenting.

For example, if the members of the project team are big picture people, don't get too deep into details. Use hot button words, lingo, and language they're familiar with.[19, 20]

Think beyond just planning to implementation. While planning is important, employees who can create, revise, administrate, and execute ideas are setting themselves up for recognition and advancement.[21]

Obviously as you become more senior at your company, you'll have picked up a lot of things. Or perhaps you bring to the table quite a bit of valuable knowledge from a long, rich career. Teach, and share what you know. There's definitely opportunity for this with new employees. Help others gain wisdom, experience, and insight.[22]

On the other hand, years of service in the same position can sometimes make one stagnant in thinking or lead to frayed attitudes with coworkers or customers. When the phone rings or that next customer approaches you, stay positive and think "opportunity," not "obligation."[23]

Don't let your attitude get worn down, and be mindful of burnout. If you feel you're getting burned out (or overloaded) but want to stay in your current position, work with your supervisor to come up with some changes that will make your work more pleasant and manageable.

Persistent or Pest?

The Marketing Director at one record label for which I worked liked my go-get-'em style and called me The Bulldog (funny also because that's the mascot of the university where I did my graduate work!). In nearly every position, your work and your success rate in meeting deadlines will (unfortunately) depend on input from other people. When you follow up, don't be such a bulldog that you tick people off or get branded a nag.

After waiting for a reasonable time, and based on the urgency of the project, remind those who are holding you up. A good sequence of touch points is: request, log, remind by email, then finally—if need be—call or drop by someone's office. When doing a drop-by, make some small talk before bringing up the project. And either ask, "Do we still need this widget to release Friday?" (and if so, mention the pending item that's holding you up), or something like, "I know you've been busy, but do you think you could email me the copy for that widget by tomorrow morning? Melanie needs it before her presentation in Phoenix."

♛ NOTE--- Come up with a tracking system to keep up with what you're waiting for; you can use things like read receipts on emails you send, a spreadsheet, or www.wonderl-ist.com.

In some cases, after a reminder or 2, you may be able to just let the item pass its deadline as a way to put the onus back on the requestor. This way a "pain point" can eventually surface, causing someone involved with the project to ask you why your part is not yet done. Then you can respond with what you're waiting for, what you've done to try to move forward, and possibly ask for that person's help getting past the holdup. Keep in mind, however, that the project manager may have a flexible delivery date for the project.

My Stephen Minister gave me some wise advice once, "Attitude and mood trump ability every time." In other words, keeping your interactions and responses pleasant and professional is more important than mowing people down to meet deadlines to avoid anyone thinking you're incompetent. And I've found that to be true most of the time. It's okay to be the person that may not hit every deadline perfectly but maintains good relationships with coworkers and customers rather than the one who makes every deadline yet nags everyone to death during the process.

Understanding Your Customer and Producing Superior Products

Whether you're selling a service, processing medical claims, or coordinating an expo for the corporate office, you are creating products as you work. Increase your indispensability by really trying to understand what your customer—internal or external—needs, and coming up with a superior end product. Then, strive to deliver that product with timeliness, positivity, and a high level of customer service.[24] Keep customers happy and always look for ways to save the company money and minimize expenses.[25]

Accomplishments

Always keep up with your accomplishments and the big recognizable clients you've worked with at each job. (Although I did not work directly with the client, the work I did for the Project Managers and Sales Managers at one large company included NASA, Texas A&M University, and Boeing. Impressive clients on a résumé can really draw attention.) A good place to do this is your Older Jobs and Additional Info document.

Your new job is most likely not the last job you will have in your career, and it's easier to keep up with accomplishments as they happen rather than trying to think back after you're no longer there. List at least 1 top accomplishment per year with each company.[26] Then you can pick and choose what to include the next time you update your résumé.

People get promoted not only because they do a good job but because they perform beyond expectations, showing they can be effective in helping their company reach tomorrow's goals. So keeping up with your accomplishments as you achieve them will also be to your benefit come performance review time. Your supervisor will have a lot on her mind all the time, so as I've said before, find little ways to sell yourself occasionally, tooting your horn without bragging. This will assure her you are working hard, getting results, and that she's chosen the best candidate for the position. And as you become more proficient at your job, ask for more responsibility. This is an indirect way to ask for a raise and can help you move up the company ladder.[27]

Workload

Some companies may not ease you into your position, and your workload may ramp up quickly after you begin. So if you have after-hours building access or can patch into the company network remotely, work some overtime in the beginning if necessary to keep up. If you are an "exempt" employee (do not get paid extra for hours you put in over 40 per week) I'd also recommend using "overtime" to complete online trainings, benefits paperwork, performance review preparation, etc.—things required by the company. Then use core hours for your regular work.

Overtime is definitely not a fun thought—especially at the beginning of a new position—but as your skills increase and you become more efficient at your job, there should be less need for it. Look at this time as a season. Plan to work hard and do more than is expected, avoiding a "that's not my job" mentality. Strive to master your primary tasks early on. Whether you started out as a temp or a mid-level manager, doing a great job will help you advance your career. Good supervisors notice, appreciate, and will want to encourage and promote their best staff.

As far as asking for more responsibility—the adding to your workload we discussed earlier—you may feel a bit overloaded already. Or when your supervisor asks if you can also handle ___ (something additional), you may be anxious or think, "I'm juggling a lot already. How can I handle *more*?" But if you really want to get ahead and become more and more valuable to the company, consider answering, "You bet!"

Feelings of apprehension are normal when it comes to more work, but feel good that your supervisor believes in you enough to have asked you to take this new thing on. Jump in with both feet and dog-paddle. Google it and figure it out as you go; then you can learn synchronized swimming and the fancy tricks later.[28]

Workaholism

A couple of articles I ran across during the writing of this book really got me thinking about something I've not had an issue with but that affects so many: workaholism. If quality of life is important to you, read on.

More professionals than ever have laptops and can access corporate networks, email, and the internet nearly anywhere. Did you know that on weekends a whopping 98% of executives log on to work email when they're not at the office? Can you believe 577 million vacation days went unused by U.S. workers in 2013? And 94% of professionals work 50+ hours per week! As I mentioned earlier, there's a time for going the extra mile as you get settled in at your new job, but too many working people are losing quality of life.

Work is an important element of life, and doing your best at your job and in the course of your career is good for everyone. However, too much work can be counterproductive. Research has shown that 2 months' worth of 60-hour work weeks were no more productive than 40-hour weeks and that in less than 1 month, 80-hour weeks caused burnout.[29]

Move toward going home on time. Limit working long hours to occasional projects that merit the time. Try to mentally detach when you leave the office. On vacation, nights, or weekends, resist that habit or temptation to respond to work emails. Don't put so much pressure on yourself that you assume your supervisor and/or coworkers *must* have everything they ask for lightning fast or that anyone will think you're a slacker if you're not working 50+ hour weeks (even if others are).

♛ NOTE--- If your job involves a lot of time at the computer, give your eyes a break and look away from your monitor for 10 seconds every 10 minutes.

Employees in Spain, France, and Brazil have an average of 30 vacation days a year, but in the U.S. and Mexico they only have 10.[29] Further, the U.S. is the only industrialized nation that doesn't require companies to give full-time employees paid vacation time![30] (Check out www.vacationequalityproject.com for a list of a few things you can do to further the movement for vacation equality in the U.S.) Finally, research by former NASA scientists found that workers show an 82% increase in job performance upon returning from a vacation. Folks, let's try to strike a better balance when it comes to how work fits into our lives. It may sound trite or cheesy, but a healthier and happier you is a better worker.[31]

RECAP:

- As soon as you land your new job, review and implement the items on the Before/During/After list in this chapter.
- Dress appropriately for the job and your position.
- Notice problems and figure out ways to solve them.
- Perception continues to be reality at this stage, so be positive, and don't show any panic you may feel.
- Watch what you say and how you say it, especially since you're the new kid on the block. Don't complain or vent to fellow employees about work, regardless of where you are.
- Think creatively, write down good ideas, and stay up on developments and news in your industry.
- Starting day 1, notice and do your best to fit in with corporate culture, developing the appropriate people skills to help you best interact with your coworkers and customers.
- Log your accomplishments at every job you have.
- Anticipate overtime for a while after you first begin, but don't feel pressured into workaholism. Strike a good balance between work and quality of life.

Other Reading:

- *Man Upstairs LifeHacks: Money - A 60-Minute Beginner's Guide to Rethinking Your Personal Finances* by Gabriel Aviles (www.manupstairs.com)

Endnotes:

1. http://www.mdmproofing.com/iym/emergency_fund.html
2. *Nashville Career Fairs Directory and Career Guide* (July, 2010): 77.
3. Right Management, "How To Work A Room," presentation (January, 2010): 1.
4. Barry Eigen, "Ways To Get Ahead In Tough Times," *Readers Digest* leaflet (1991).
5. Barry Eigen, "Ways To Get Ahead In Tough Times," *Readers Digest* leaflet (1991).
6. Patrick Erwin, "Bulletproof Your Job: 4 Ways to Stay Employed" CareerBuilder.com article
7. Patrick Erwin, "Bulletproof Your Job: 4 Ways to Stay Employed" CareerBuilder.com article
8. http://images.gmimage3.com/members/10868/ftp/publications/Are%20You%20Indispensible%20At%20Work.pdf
9. Robert B. Tucker, "Are You Indispensable at Work," *MPI Northern California Chapter Perspective* 28, no. 6 (June, 2010): 9.
10. http://images.gmimage3.com/members/10868/ftp/publications/Are%20You%20Indispensible%20At%20Work.pdf
11. http://www.inc.com/jeff-haden/9-sensational-traits-of-highly-promotable-employees.html
12. Patrick Erwin, "Bulletproof Your Job: 4 Ways to Stay Employed" CareerBuilder.com article
13. *Nashville Career Fairs Directory and Career Guide* (July, 2010): 77.
14. Patrick Erwin, "Bulletproof Your Job: 4 Ways to Stay Employed" CareerBuilder.com article

15. *Nashville Career Fairs Directory and Career Guide* (July, 2010): 77.

16. Barry Eigen, "Ways To Get Ahead In Tough Times," *Readers Digest* leaflet (1991).

17. Rodney Laughlin, *Getting the Job: A Guide For Employment Seekers* (1987): 34.

18. Patrick Erwin, "Bulletproof Your Job: 4 Ways to Stay Employed" CareerBuilder.com article

19. Robert B. Tucker, "Are You Indispensable at Work," *MPI Northern California Chapter Perspective* 28, no. 6 (June, 2010): 9.

20. Patrick Erwin, "Bulletproof Your Job: 4 Ways to Stay Employed" CareerBuilder.com article

21. http://www.inc.com/jeff-haden/9-sensational-traits-of-highly-promotable-employees. html

22. http://www.inc.com/jeff-haden/9-sensational-traits-of-highly-promotable-employees. html

23. http://images.gmimage3.com/members/10868/ftp/publications/Are%20You%20 Indispensible%20At%20Work.pdf

24. http://images.gmimage3.com/members/10868/ftp/publications/Are%20You%20 Indispensible%20At%20Work.pdf

25. Patrick Erwin, "Bulletproof Your Job: 4 Ways to Stay Employed" CareerBuilder.com article

26. Right Management, "Interviewing Strategies," presentation (January, 2010): 2.

27. Barry Eigen, "Ways To Get Ahead In Tough Times," *Readers Digest* leaflet (1991).

28. Barry Eigen, "Ways To Get Ahead In Tough Times," *Readers Digest* leaflet (1991).

29. Tom Foster, "Are You A Workaholic?" *Details* (October 2014): 140-145.

30. Christine Birkner, "The Right to R&R" Marketing News (November 2014): 12.

31. Tom Foster, "Are You A Workaholic?" *Details* (October 2014): 140-145.

EPILOGUE

Hope, Encouragement, and Purpose

On a personal note, I'd like to share a few things from my heart. I fully respect everyone's beliefs, and I know this section may offend some people or step on some toes. We're all in different places with religion and our spiritual journey, but I would be remiss to end this book without including the following content. Why keep to myself what has been so encouraging and helpful to me?

♛ NOTE--- God has a purpose for your pain, a reason for your struggle, and a gift for your faithfulness. Don't give up! –Unknown

There are so many great spiritual resources that have encouraged me through times of job transition that I felt some of them should be included in this book. If you're not a Christian, feel free to skip over portions of this section. But I would encourage you—and it doesn't have to be today—to just take in this section with an open mind. No pressure. Learn about the character of God and how He fits into your life and job search. Make up your own mind.

Losing your job is one of the most significant negative events you can experience. To say the time between a job loss and landing your next job is challenging is an understatement. Since most of us draw much of our identity from our work, this time can break you down to the core of who you are and cause you to question yourself.

You will have your fair share of pity parties and may experience depression. Seasons of career transition can tend to amplify other challenges you're dealing with (romance, family, health), increasing stress. And the not knowing where or when you'll land, combined with the period of waiting, will tend to weigh you down, stress you out, or downright make you crazy sometimes. Believe me, I know!

Career transition—even if you *do* have a job now and are seeking another—is rarely easy. I always say it's a season that can turn you to God. I don't know how those who don't have a personal relationship with God, and have Him to turn to, make it through the process.

My friends and family, the Scripture I read, the literature I take in, and being able to be real, raw, and honest with God give me strength. There's relevance and synergy between job transition and the spiritual strength you can draw from your relationship with God. That's why I wanted to include this section.

The first thing I want to include calms me down at the beginning of my career transitions and is an excellent first read after a layoff—if that is your situation. Thanks to the author for her permission to reprint.

PERSPECTIVE: "A DIVINE HOLIDAY" BY MARLANE PEAK

"So do not fear, for I am with you; do not be dismayed, for I am your God. I will strengthen you and help you; I will uphold you with my righteous right hand." Isaiah 41:10.

As I read this passage the morning of April 20, the words seemed to jump off the page and speak to my heart in a very personal way—especially the phrase, "do not be dismayed." I wondered, "What does God have in store for me today?" Little did I know how much I would need this encouragement a few hours later when my manager called me into her office and told me my position was being eliminated, and I could get my things and go home.

I was devastated. I had been with the organization for 10 years and believed in their mission and values. I was single with all the financial responsibility on my shoulders, had a son in college, and no family to fall back on—which made matters worse. Friends gathered around me that evening offering support and listening to my fears and pain. As they left, I asked if they could give me a positive vision for the future. Unfortunately, they were at a loss for words, and I was left dreading the days and weeks ahead.

To get my mind off my troubles, I arranged to meet a friend at a movie the next afternoon. I arrived at the theater early and looked for a place to sit. Amazingly, there was only one bench in the lobby, and a rather odd-looking lady was sitting there with a package beside her. I hesitated to ask if I could take the empty space, but I was tired and wanted to rest. When I asked if I could sit next to her, she smiled a big smile and said, "Sure." We began to have small talk about waiting for friends and where we lived. I asked her where she worked, and she replied she had recently been laid off. I was amazed we were in the same position; however, I was soon to find out we had very different perspectives on what this meant.

"I am not worried," she continued, "I look on it as a 'Divine Holiday.' Do you know how many people got up today and wished they didn't have to go to work? I got to sleep in and meet a friend at the movie! You know if you trust God, you don't have to worry. When He is ready, He will bring the job. So I am going to enjoy this time off because I know at the right time, God is going to bring me another job. My brother was just laid off, and he is so stressed out he is making his wife and kids miserable. I tried to tell him if he would just trust God he wouldn't have to worry, but he won't listen to me. He is very anxious and depressed, and his whole family is suffering. Not me; I am going to enjoy my divine holiday."

It was at this moment I expected her to begin glowing as the characters in the TV show "Touched By An Angel" did when they were delivering a message from God. It was so powerful and poignant. I replied, "You are not going to believe this, but I lost my job yesterday." Somehow I felt she already knew. I continued, "I asked my friends to help give me a hopeful picture of my future, and they were unable to. However, you have just done that for me, and I am so grateful!"

"Good," she said, and the next thing I knew, her friend had arrived, and she was on her way. I watched to make sure she actually walked into the movie instead of floating up to heaven!

For the next few months, I reminded myself often of the words from this "angel"—if I trust God, I don't have to worry. Look for job – yes, but worry – no. He would bring it at His perfect time. I knew that I wanted to be a trainer in a nonprofit faith-based organization, but I didn't know how I would find it. I didn't have to—God did it for me. On June 20, exactly two months after my job had been eliminated, a nonprofit Christian organization offered me the position of Corporate Trainer. My new manager wrote in the offer letter, "God's timing is so perfect."

My divine holiday is coming to an end, but I have learned some valuable lessons while enjoying it.

- Don't be afraid to sit by strange looking people—they may have an important message for you from God.
- If you trust God, you don't have to worry.
- God keeps His promises.

WHO IS GOD IN ALL THIS, AND CAN HE HELP ME?

Once, during one of my transition periods, I asked my pastor if he felt like God was punishing me with unemployment. He said something to the effect of, "We've all sinned. We all deserve death, but we don't get what we deserve. If God had everyone who sinned lose their job, the world would be in even worse shape. That's not how He is."

Though it may feel like He's got it in for you and you're being chastised for something, resist that lie. I grew up in church, and about 10 years ago I just felt like I didn't do enough to make God happy and that every slip-up or sin made him angry. I had to break free from the "God as a cosmic punisher" mentality. God doesn't treat me as my sins deserve (Ps 103:10-11). He's long-suffering and patient (Jer 15:15) and does not oppress (Job 37:23). And although we all make Him angry at times, His anger is temporary, but His favor lasts a lifetime (Ps 30:5).

God loves and cares about you. He wants you to turn these worries and concerns over to Him... and trust Him—so easily said but tougher to do—myself included! To begin trusting God, you need to first know who He is. Read though the characteristics below (and look up the Scriptures if you like) for a good picture of the character of God. I've paraphrased these in first person, since reading them that way makes it more personable and applicable to you and what you're going through.

GOD...

IS GRACIOUS AND COMPASSIONATE
- Is gracious and compassionate (Ps 111:4)

- Is longing to be gracious and compassionate to me (Is 30:18)
- Has compassion on me (because I fear him) (Ps 103:13)

IS FAITHFUL
- Bears my burdens daily (Ps 68:19)
- Is faithful to all His promises and loving to me (Ps 117:2, 145:13)
- Does not disappoint me because I hope in Him (Is 49:23)

KNOWS, CARES, AND ANSWERS
- Sees my affliction and knows my anguish (Ps 31:7)
- Answers me when I seek Him and delivers me from all my fears (Ps 34:4)
- Will respond to and not be irritated by the prayer of the destitute (Ps 65:5, 102:17; Is 38:5)
- Cares for those who trust in Him (Nah 1:7)

LOVES ME
- Shows love to 1,000 generations who love Him and keep His commands (Deu 5:10)
- Surrounds me with His love (Ps 32:10)
- Loves me because He sent Jesus to die that I might live (Jn 3:16, 4:9)

WANTS TO GIVE ME GOOD THINGS
- Blesses the righteous and surrounds them with favor like a shield (Ps 5:12)
- Is a sun and shield, bestows favor and honor, and doesn't withhold good things from the blameless (Ps 84:11)
- Satisfies the hungry and thirsty with good things (Ps 107:9)
- Wants me to prosper and to give me hope (Jer 29:11)
- Will reward me because I seek Him earnestly (Heb 11:6)

HELPS AND DELIVERS ME
- Is loving and faithful toward those who keep His covenant (Ps 25:10)
- Delivers me from troubles (Ps 34:7, 18-19, 39-40)
- Saves and helps me (Ps 94:17)
- Guards my life (Ps 97:10)
- Comes to the aid of those doing right (Is 64:5)

WILL GIVE ME STRENGTH
- Gives power and strength to His people (Ps 68:35)
- Has nothing that is too difficult for Him (Jer 32:27)
- Will keep me strong (I Cor 1:8)
- Is faithful and will strengthen and protect me (2 Thes 3:3)

I like what speaker, author, and former executive at Financial Peace University (Dave Ramsey's organization) Jon Acuff said when I heard him speak: "We know God can part the Red Sea, heal the sick, raise people from the dead, and die for our sins, but we doubt He's powerful enough to help us with our job search. Don't undersize God." So again—easier said than done—constantly remind yourself of who He is and how He feels toward you; believe!

♛ NOTE--- It's not an easy piece of encouragement to hear, but keep in mind the more no's you get as you progress through you job search, the closer you are to a yes and landing your next position.

WE'VE ALL THOUGHT ABOUT IT

As private and ugly a thought as suicide is, I think everyone entertains the option—especially during an extended job search or times when they are not experiencing positive results from their efforts or are receiving a lot of rejections. Here are some ways that have helped me fend off these negative thoughts.

Make a list of what you're thankful for—what you *do* have and the things that *are* going right for you currently. Think about what you've accomplished today, who you helped or plan to help, what made you happy today, and anything you're looking forward to next (e.g., dinner with friends, that vacation or holiday party, buying something from your wish list). This should help get you into a more positive frame of mind.

Hang in there. Sometimes getting that right job takes longer than we'd all like because it's a matter of timing. Perhaps the job is not quite open yet because, for example, the person in it now hasn't been promoted or left to be a full-time mom.

Take comfort in the fact that God may need you somewhere new now, to encourage or help others or to bless your new employer with your skills, knowledge, and experience. Maybe you're a high-level (C-suite) manager who'll be brought in to completely change a location's culture for the better.

Remember, regardless of your work situation or anything else that's a burden on your mind during this time, your friends and your family still need you. Say it out loud: "People... *need*... me."

Fact, faith, and feelings—I remember years ago as a youth seeing *The Four Spiritual Laws* tract. Simple as it may seem, the analogy is a train. Fact is the engine, so regardless of your feelings, remember the facts and what your actual situation is without a lens of drama or worry. Your feelings are a section of the train, the caboose. But a train can run without a caboose. So although your feelings are a part of the equation, remember Fact is out front, Faith knits it together, and Feelings are last. Put your faith in what God has promised in Scripture and in His trustworthiness.[1]

Journal—whether it's a paper journal or just making a new document for each day you write, journaling is a healthy and effective way to pour out your sadness, frustration, thoughts, disappointments, joys, etc. This is not only cathartic, but it can be a means of sorting out your feelings and thoughts. Further, most times you can figure out a solution to what's bothering you. As much as I can, I try to end the journal entry with what is going right or well, stating the key thoughts I've distilled out of that journal entry, and/or the things I'm thankful for.

List the good things about yourself. As stated earlier, most people derive self-worth and identity from their job. And that's to be expected. Heck, it's one of the first things someone you've just met asks you about, not to mention where you spend a majority of your time! So in seasons when you're not working, it's easy to forget your value outside of a job. Shoot for 5 good things about yourself… I bet you can come up with 10! These can be personal traits and/or about yourself as an employee. Consider your strengths, things for which others have complimented you, etc. You can even ask a close friend or 2 for their take on what your strengths are.

You never know what awesome thing is to come, personally or in your work situation! For example, I never thought I'd be able to travel internationally until one of the music dot-coms I worked for closed down. We got 3 full months of pay and some other great things in our severance packages. Then. in just a few weeks, I got a new job under my former supervisor at the next company he moved to, so I didn't really spend much of the severance package and was later able to use those funds for a trip to London, Paris, and Amsterdam. I've gotten to do several other amazing international trips, songwrite with some of my favorite artists, buy a house without debt or a mortgage, write this book, and on and on. Think back over your life to some things you'd have never believed would happen if someone told you 20 years ago.

Seeing your pastor or a Stephen Minister can definitely be a no-cost way of having a shoulder to lean on and discuss thoughts, etc. that are too weighty to express to a friend. Search the web, or call a large local church to see if they can help connect you. Again, hang in there. This is a season, and better days are soon to come.

LET THE MUSIC MOVE YOU

Now for something fun! I'm a music guy. I love singing, writing, and producing music—kinda fell into it after moving to Nashville to just work on the business side of the industry. Regardless, I've always been a huge music fan. As a kid, I remember listening to pop radio on a portable radio in my tree house (which was actually just a piece of Formica-board nailed onto a branch up in a pine tree) near my home in Mississippi. The 6 songs below specifically encouraged me during my last several job searches, so I wanted to recommend listening to them (you can find them and a few others at www.kurtkirton.com) as well as reading the lyrics (links to the lyrics follow the titles below.)

1. Kathleen Carnali's "I Will Not Be Afraid" - http://bit.ly/kciwnba
2. Farrell & Farrell's "Find the Way to Love" - http://bit.ly/ffftwtl
3. Danny Gokey's "Hope in Front of Me" - http://bit.ly/dghifom
4. Kutless' "What Faith Can Do" - http://bit.ly/kwhatfaith
5. Mandisa's "Overcomer" - http://bit.ly/movercomer
6. Plumb's "I Can't Do This" - http://bit.ly/picdt

THE 20 COMMANDMENTS

I stumbled on this list a while back. I don't "get" all the points below, but there is some good insight.

1. If you feel far away from God, guess who moved?
2. Fear knocked. Faith answered. No one was there.

3. What you are is God's gift to you. What you become is your gift to God.
4. I am God's melody of life, and He sings His song through me.
5. We can never really go where God is not; and where He is, all is well.
6. No matter what is happening in your life, know that God is waiting for you with open arms.
7. God promises a safe landing, not a calm passage.
8. Do your best, and then sleep in peace. God is awake.
9. God has a purpose and plan for you that no one else can fulfill.
10. The will of God will never take you to where the Grace of God will not protect you.
11. We are responsible for the effort, not the outcome.
12. We set the sail. God makes the wind.
13. Begin to weave, and God will give you the thread.
14. When God says, "No," it's because He has something better in store for you.
15. The task ahead of us is never as great as the Power behind us.
16. Prayer: Don't bother to give God instructions, just report for duty.
17. It's my business to do God's business, and it's His business to take care of my business.
18. Serenity is not freedom from the storm but peace amidst the storm.
19. How come we're always running around looking for God? He's not lost.
20. God put me on earth to accomplish a number of things. Right now, I'm so far behind I will live forever!

– Author Unknown

Numbers 4, 7, and 13 bring to mind some thoughts:

#4 - My sister told me once (and I think she does better with this than I do) that God can use you to encourage someone—every day—if you just keep your eyes open to opportunities. I usually tear up every time I think about this. It doesn't have to be a big heavy conversation or giving a homeless guy $20. It could be just listening to someone share the pain they're currently going through with a child, smiling at someone at the gas station who looks worried, or saying a kind word to someone who's a jerk to you at work. You know the old saying, "You're the only Jesus some may ever see." Look for the opportunity to bless someone every day—whether you're in transition or working.

#7 - Wow, ain't that the truth. If only it wasn't so painful and complicated to get to that safe landing area in life! I wish. But y'know, if I hadn't been through everything I have in my career, I wouldn't be writing this book. If countless musicians hadn't had painful relationships, we'd be without hundreds—maybe thousands—of hit songs. And I think back to 2 Cor 1:4 ("[God]...comforts us in all our troubles, so that we can comfort those in any trouble with the comfort we ourselves have received from God.") Sometimes difficult circumstances are our fault, but sometimes God allows some challenging miserable times into our lives so we can have the experience in order to encourage others down the road, be their shoulder to lean on, and share encouragement and wise empathetic advice.

#13 - If this doesn't apply to the job search, I don't know what does! At first, the loss of your job is so emotional and overwhelming. *"What happened? Why? What do I do now? Where will I end up, and what will happen to me?"* But if you can just start, take baby steps (corny as it may seem, remember the Bill Murray movie *What About Bob?*), God will support you, guide you, and come up under and beside you to give you the strength to move forward and keep going. Reading this book is a good start, too, since it is also helpful to have something practical as a guide. Once I expressed to Richard, a pastor friend of mine, that I was not sure which decision to make sometimes in my job search and was afraid of getting outside the will of God. I like his response. He said, "God has given us a brain and our wits, and we should use them to make the best decisions we can along the way." Sometimes there are things you risk or gamble, like stalling on that one solid job offer while hoping the amazing position you're waiting for will come through. Be humble; be mindful of following His will; and trust God to "give you the thread" and get you to the right job.

And that line of thought, as well as #8 in the list above, are a great segue into the piece below.

A MESSAGE FROM PASTOR CINDY ANDREWS-LOOPER

Pastor Cindy Andrews-Looper (former pastor of Holy Trinity Church in Nashville, TN) would send out a regular email to those on her church's subscriber list. What a great encouragement when it comes to job search worries. Printed with permission:

"Not to us, O Lord, not to us, but to Your name be the glory, because of Your love and faithfulness." Psalm 115:1

We sing a praise chorus in worship that includes the words from the above Psalm. And today, those words have been ringing in my soul.

The last pastor's corner I sent out was on Friday, August 30th. Jen and I had worked long hours to get our house ready to put on the market. I shared with you how utterly exhausted we were. I told you that I sensed God speaking to me to let it go. I had done all that I could do, and now it was time for Him to take over. I tried to be intentional about releasing my anxiety. I would envision myself lying back in a pool and floating. This has for a long time been the visual that God uses to show me to trust Him.

On Sunday, September 1, we had our first open house. By Wednesday, September 4th, we had a contract on the house for the asking price! We were so amazed and thankful for God's faithfulness. For God had once again showed us that after we have done our part, we can trust Him to do His part. This week, we put a contract on a condo that we love in the Bellevue area. We will close on our current house and the condo on October 4th. Over the coming weeks, we will be packing, going through everything to downsize and having a huge yard sale this coming Friday and Saturday. We still have much to do. But today, I am filled with such joy and security over the faithfulness of God for His children.

I often preach that you can trust God. And every time I am faced with circumstances in which I must trust Him, He is always faithful in doing His part. The key, I have found, is doing your part and then giving it to Him. However, you can't expect Him to do His part if you aren't willing to do your part. You see, God works with us to bring about good and blessings in our lives. He is our high and holy Partner in this journey of life. In every situation that we face, there are things we can and should be doing. And when we have done those, we must release the situation into God's hands. We must ask Him to take over and do what we cannot do.

Some of you are reading this, and you have been filled with anxiety. You have not been sleeping. Your mind has been going nonstop as you try to figure out the situation that lies before you. I want to first ask you a question: As you look at this situation, have you done everything that you can do? If there are still things that you can do, then I recommend that you do your part. However, if you know you have done everything you can do, it is time to release this situation into God's hands. Let it go! Back away from it! Give it to Him, and trust Him to do His part.

I think God will sometimes wait to see if we are going to give the situation to Him. He watches us anxiously trying to figure things out. He sees us losing sleep over it. And He so longs to have us say, "God, here, I have done everything I can do. Please take this, and do Your part." And when we release it, the Holy Spirit begins a work within us, around the situation and within other individuals involved in the situation. We can lie back and rest in God's love and grace. And if we do that, we will see the handiwork of God's perfect timing. The situation will begin to change and transform as the almighty power of God intervenes on our behalf.

I challenge you today to look at the situations in your life that seem bigger than you right now. Ask yourself if you have done everything that you can do. If not, then do what you need to do. If so, then release it to God, and rest. God's desire is to take care of you. He wants to show you that He is, indeed, your Heavenly and Holy Parent who is faithful in His love and grace.

Today, I end by giving all thanks and praise to God Most High for hearing our prayer and doing His part in the journey before us! God is faithful! You can count on Him in every situation. He loves you and so wants to show you just how He can and will take care of you. But before you are going to see that, you must do your part, and then let it go! To God be the glory!

"I proclaim righteousness in the great assembly; I do not seal my lips. I do not hide Your righteousness in my heart; I speak of Your faithfulness and salvation. I do not conceal your love and your truth from the great assembly." Psalm 40:9-10

I love you all and I look forward to seeing you on Sunday! Hugs and prayers!

–Pastor Cindy

THE PARABLE OF THE PENCIL

The Pencil Maker took the pencil aside, and just before putting him into the box said, "There are 5 things you need to know before I send you out into the world. Always remember them; never forget; and you will become the best pencil you can be."

1. You will be able to do many great things but only if you allow yourself to be held in someone's hand.
2. You will experience a painful sharpening from time to time, but you'll need it to become a better pencil.
3. You will be able to correct any mistakes you might make.
4. The most important part of you will always be what's inside.
5. On every surface you are used on, you must leave your mark. No matter what the condition, you must continue to write.

The pencil understood, promised to remember, and went into the box with purpose in its heart. Now replace the pencil with you. Always remember these things; never forget; and you will become the best person you can be.

1. You will be able to do many great things, but only if you allow yourself to be held in God's hand—and allow other human beings to access you for the many gifts you possess.
2. You will experience a painful sharpening from time to time by going through various problems in life, but you'll need it to become a stronger person.
3. You will be able to correct any mistakes you might make.
4. The most important part of you will always be what's on the inside.
5. On every surface you walk across, you must leave your mark. No matter what the situation, you must continue to do your duties.

Allow this parable of the pencil to encourage you to know that you are a special person, and only you can fulfill the purpose you were born to accomplish. Never allow yourself to get discouraged and think that your life is insignificant and cannot make a change.

–Author Unknown

SCRIPTURAL ENCOURAGEMENT

And finally, read through the Scripture below. Moreover, I encourage you to highlight and commit to memory the verses that are the most encouraging to you. This way, you can recall them when you don't have them in front of you. A document of these scriptures is available in the downloadable zip file alongside the templates and scripts.

HOPE

Lam 3:21-23	[because of this] I have hope: Because of the Lord's great love, we are not consumed, for His compassions never fail. They are new every morning. Great is your faithfulness.
Jas 1:12	Blessed is the man who perseveres under trial.
Jer 29:11	For I know the plans I have for you says the Lord...plans to prosper you and not to harm you...to give you a hope and a future.
Heb 10:23	Let us hold unswervingly to the hope we profess, for He who has promised is faithful.
Php 4:19	My God will meet all your needs according to His glorious riches in Christ Jesus.
Rom 8:25	But if I hope for what I do not yet have, I wait for it patiently.
Jn 10:10	...I have come that they may have life and have it to the full.
Ps 37:4	Delight yourself in the Lord, and He will give you the desires of your heart.
Ps 55:22	Cast your cares on the Lord, and He will sustain you; He will never let the righteous fall.
Ps 54:4	Surely God is my help; the Lord is the one who sustains me.
Is 55:8	"For my thoughts are not your thoughts, neither are your ways my ways," declares the Lord.
Rom 5:3-5	...sufferings...produce...hope. And hope does not disappoint us, because God has poured out His love into our hearts by the Holy Spirit that He has given us.
2 Cor 4:8	We are hard pressed on every side, but not crushed; perplexed but not in despair.
Mt 21:22	If you believe, you will receive whatever you ask for in prayer.
Pr 16:9 & 33	In his heart a man plans his course, but the Lord determines his steps. The lot is cast into the lap, but its every decision is from the Lord.
Ps 37:18-19	The blameless spend their days under the Lord's care, and their inheritance will endure forever. In times of disaster they will not wither; in days of famine they will enjoy plenty.
Ps 18:19	He brought me out into a spacious place; He rescued me because He delighted in me.
Ecc 8:6-7 & 15	There is a proper time and procedure for every matter, though a man's misery weighs heavily upon him. Since no man knows the future, who can tell him what is to come? So I commend the enjoyment of life, because nothing is better for a man under the sun than to eat and drink and be glad. Then joy will accompany him in his work all the days of the life God has given him under the sun.
Ps 138:7b	Though I walk in the midst of trouble, You preserve my life...

ENCOURAGEMENT

Is 46:4	I have made you, and I will carry you; I will sustain you, and I will rescue you.
Ps 28:7	The Lord is my strength and my shield; my heart trusts in Him and I am helped.
Ps 18:32	It is God who arms me with strength and makes my way perfect.
Prov 3:5-6	Trust in the Lord with all your heart. Lean not on your own understanding. In all your ways acknowledge Him...He will direct your paths.
Ps 143:8	Let the morning bring me word of your unfailing love, for I have put my trust in you. Show me the way I should go, for to you I lift up my soul.
I Pet 4:12-13	Do not be surprised at the painful trial you are suffering as though something strange were happening to you. But rejoice that you participate in the sufferings of Christ so that you may be overjoyed when His glory is revealed.
Ps 119:116	Sustain me according to your promise, and I will live; do not let my hopes be dashed.
2 Cor 12:9	"My grace is sufficient for you, for my power is made perfect in weakness."
Ps 22:24	For He has not despised or disdained the suffering of the afflicted one; He has not hidden His face from him but has listened to his cry for help.
Ecc 11:5	As you do not know the path of the wind, or how the body is formed in a mother's womb, so you cannot understand the work of God, the Maker of all things.
Mt 21:21	"...if you have faith and do not doubt...you can say to this mountain, 'Go throw your self into the sea,' and it will be done."
Ps 62:8	Trust in Him at all times, O people; pour out your hearts to Him, for God is our refuge.
Php 4:6	Do not be anxious about anything, but in everything by prayer and petition with thanksgiving, present your requests to God.
Php 4:13	I can do all things through Christ who strengthens me.
Prov 19:21	Many are the plans in a man's heart, but it is the Lord's purpose that prevails.
Is 41:10	So do not fear, for I am with you; do not be dismayed for I am your God. I will strengthen you and help you. I will uphold you with my hand.
Jn 14:27	Peace I leave with you; my peace I give you. I do not give to you as the world gives. Do not let your hearts be troubled, and do not be afraid.
Ps 32:8	I will instruct you and teach you in the way you should go; I will counsel you and watch over you.
Ps 112:6-7	...a righteous man...will have no fear of bad news; his heart is steadfast, trusting in the Lord.
Ps 34:19	A righteous man may have many troubles, but the Lord delivers him from them all.
Mt 6:25a	...do not worry about your life...

Ps 56:3	When I am afraid, I will trust in You.
Ps 115:11	You who fear Him, trust in the Lord—He is your help and shield.
Ps 31:3, 7, 9, 23	Since you are my rock and my fortress, for the sake of your name, lead and guide me. I will be glad and rejoice in your love, for you saw my affliction and knew the anguish of my soul. Be merciful to me, O Lord, for I am in distress; my eyes grow weak with sorrow, my soul and my body with grief. ...the Lord preserves the faithful.

IF THIS IS A LITTLE NEW TO YOU

If you do not have a personal relationship with God, if you have never consciously prayed to renounce your old life and accept Christ as your personal savior, some of this chapter may not make complete sense to you. You may have questions. You may have been to church on and off over the course of your life. You may have talked to family, friends, or seen TV preachers talk about salvation. Or you might have seen *The Passion of the Christ* on DVD. First, let me say thank you for being open minded and reading this far. Second, I must say that I believe that the Bible is God's message to us. And that's what this section of the book has been based on.

Here's my story. My parents thought it was a good idea to "send the kids to church," so I grew up "in the church." I went to Sunday School and children's church before getting into youth group and "big church" in junior high. I sang the songs, listened to the pastors, and knew a lot. But it took a while to realize that knowing is different from accepting and experiencing. That dawned on me when I was 14, and I "got saved" (or received Christ into my life).

I was a gung-ho kid for God and stepped on a lot of toes! I remember offending our one and only neighbor after feeling convicted to finally share the gospel with her—but did it over the phone (ugh!) (She lived across the street.) But I've realized that we all become wiser as we age, not that we're ever perfect; it's just that as we experience more and more as life goes on, we have more wisdom and better perspective.

"Where are you going with all this?" you might be wondering. I just want to say that it's not about which religion is "the one" or whose church is right or any of the things that have divided Protestants into denominations. It all comes down to the fact that God made you, and He loves you. He wants to have a relationship with you—even more than that one person you recall that you thought was amazing, the one that you *loved* and they loved you back, and for a time, it was heaven. Think that love—but thousands of times stronger. That's how God feels about you.

And since He feels that way about you, He had to make a way past your sin to get to you and did so through Jesus, His son. Take a few minutes and read through this information for a deeper explanation - http://bit.ly/fsitbnow.

So that page talks about praying a simple prayer. If you are wondering what to pray, I think it would look something like this:

> *"Dear God, (insert whatever your relationship with or knowledge of Him has been thus far), but I confess and repent of my sins. I believe that you sent Christ to die for my sins so You could know and have a relationship with me. I accept You into my heart and life and receive Your salvation. Make me a new creature as You promised in your Word. Cleanse me; save me from the path I was on, and guide me from here on out. Amen."*

Although this book was not meant to be a funnel to the gospel or direct anyone to do anything with his or her spiritual life, it wouldn't make much sense to share the encouragement in this section of the book but omit mentioning salvation and how to really experience it.

If you just prayed that prayer, I'm sure you have some new questions. Find a church you're comfortable with that believes and speaks the truth according to the Bible. Ask for help learning more about what to do and where to go from here. (The church you choose may call this "getting discipled.") Start reading the Bible through at the book of Matthew, the first book of the New Testament. These things will give you knowledge and start you on the road to maturing spiritually (a never ending process!).

Blessings to you spiritually and in your job search. Be encouraged, and keep pressing on.

Endnote:

1. http://theworddetective.wordpress.com/tag/the-four-spiritual-laws-train

Other Reading:

- *When the Rains Fall: Trusting God When Things Look Impossible* by Bob Farrell
- *Thank God It's Monday: Ministry In The Workplace* by Mark Greene
- *Journey to Sunrise: Christian Guide to Career Transition* by Clark Liddell (This is a free online program based on the author's personal journey of self-discovery during his 14-month career transition - www.journeytosunrise.com.)
- *The Grace Awakening* by Charles Swindoll

ACKNOWLEDGEMENTS

Big thanks to:
Ash Awan
Heather Baker
Wynn Batson
Jason Bean
Jason Beetz
Heath Bertram
Caryn Chebira
Dave Delaney
JJ DiUbaldi
Jamie Dunham
Dan Faber
Clay Faircloth
Bob & Jayne Farrell
Mark Fentriss
Hal Hassal
Brett Henley
Stephanie Huffman & the Epiphany Creative Services team
Regan Jones
Matt LeBlanc
Carol Marion
John McKennon
Jennifer Miller
Jennifer Nash
Mark Newsom
Ric Pepin
Cathy Robinson
Stew Ross
William Shea
Walter Tieck
Denny Upkins
Nancy VanReece
...and my mother and sister for always being so supportive of my talents and endeavors

APPENDIX

All the documents that follow are available for download at
www.kurtkirton.com/hthtfiles.zip

BACKDOOR EMAIL

Dear ____:
After having seen the posting for the ____ position ___ (the company) is seeking to fill, I just applied online. In addition, I wanted to make sure my résumé and cover letter are seen by someone in the ____ department. If you are not the hiring manager for this position, I would appreciate it if you would forward this email to him or her. Thank you very much for your time and help.

Sincerely,

((your name here))

NOTE: If it's the case, you can open like this:

Hi John:
Carol Jones at ABC Company gave me your name as someone who might be able to help me. After having seen…

COMPANY INFO

Ricardo Montero	**Tango Press -** 617 Murfreesboro Pike Phoenix, AZ
999-7118	rmontero@tpress.com
	Owner
Interview:	7/7/15 - 3:30
Position:	Graphic Designer

Facts:
- Opened in 2000
- Main business is manufacturing of glue
- President is Bubba Wigglesworth
- Wal-Mart and Target are its primary customers

Anticipate Being Asked, and Prepare for:
- Why do you want to work for us/want this job?
- Why should we hire you/what can you do for us?
- Where do you see yourself in 5 (10, etc.) years?
- Why did you leave/are you leaving your last position?
- Tell me about yourself.
- How do you feel your skills are adaptable and will benefit us?

Questions for the Interviewer:
- Is this a new position, or replacing someone who left?
- What is the process you will be following to make a hiring decision?
- What do you think are the greatest challenges in this position?
- What skills and personality traits do you think are important for someone in this position?
- To whom do I report?
- (If the interviewer will be your supervisor) How would you describe your management style?
- How does the company encourage and reward innovative thinking, ideas, and implementation?
- How much travel will be involved?
- Who will be training?
- When would you like to have the new position filled?
- What are the hours/days of work?
- When/what is the next step (When will you be deciding 2nd Interviews/when should I expect to hear back from you)?
- Is it alright to follow up with you ___ (date)?

Some personal questions about the interviewer:
- Are you from ___ (state) originally?
- How often do you ___ run marathons? (hobby)

FUTURE POSITION COVER LETTER

Willamina Costa
119 Dew St.
Bucksnort, TN 37140

April 22, 2015

Mr. Craig Sanderson
VP of Marketing
Cirrius Marketing Group
25 Sky View Ave.
Bucksnort, TN 37140

Dear Mr. Sanderson:

After seeing how your company serves its customers from management consulting to social media marketing, I'm confident my skills could be a great asset there.

Be it online, print, television, or radio, I have helped my customers meet their goals for branding and exposure—from establishing initial marketing plans to implementing national ad campaigns. Further, I've been successful coordinating people and establishing procedure to complete projects by deadline.

I am currently seeking a Marketing or creative Project Management position. My résumé is attached. Please let me know if you hear of anything that might be a good fit or have such an opening arise at Cirrius. Thank you very much.

Sincerely,

Willamina Costa
willaminac.com/resume.html
(615) 555-1212

HEADHUNTERS, JOB SEARCH FIRMS, TEMP AGENCIES LOG

HEADHUNTERS, JOB SEARCH FIRMS, TEMP AGENCIES

FIRST TIME CALLING SCRIPT: Hi. I'm ____ (your name), referred by ____. [Elevator Speech.] Do you do any placement for ____ jobs? Could we meet? OR: What is the next step?

STATUS	COMPANY	PHONE	CONTACT	Do they place jobs	EMAIL ADDRESS	NOTES
HEADHUNTERS/JOB SEARCH FIRMS:						
4/1 - follow up.	Omishakin & Associates - 452	800-123-0001	Teresa Brinton	Yes; No fee	tbrinton@oassociates.com	Great and funny lady, very much an advocate for me. Found via career transition group blas
6/1 - follow up.	FiveChairs Talent/Mark News	615-504-8534	Phylis Harrell	Yes; No fee	info@fivechairs.com	www.fivechairs.com. They don't meet in person—phone only. Reply to their 1st em w/ my rë
TEMP AGENCIES:						
4/1 - follow up.	Randstad - 321 Electric Ave.	999-123-1000	Mallorie Wisnant	Places for Temp, Perm	mwisnant@us.randstad.com	She says she has all my contact info
6/1 - follow up.	Express - 2210 Rosa L Parks	999-123-1001	Marcy Hanson	Places for mostly tem	mhanson@expresspros.com	Go to expresspros.com & update my info/if probs call 800-222-4057
6/1 - follow up.	Staffmark - 2312 Lebanon Rd	999-123-1002	Jo Beaumont	Does mainly admin s	jb@staffmark.com	www.staffmark.com

INTERVIEW THANK-YOU LETTER

Lara Pinkleton
11 Terabyte Dr.
Las Vegas, NV 89102

May 15, 2015

Angela Martinez
Impact, Inc.
523 Blue Chip Dr.
Las Vegas, NV 89105

Dear Angela:

Thank you again for the opportunity to meet with you Friday about the **Marketing Specialist** position. The position we discussed is the type of challenge on which I thrive, and I am confident I can meet—if not exceed—your goals. I am impressed with your company and very interested in working with Impact, Inc. I will follow up with you in a few weeks.

Sincerely,

Lara Pinkleton

JOB APPLICATION FOLLOW UP LETTER

Lara Pinkleton
11 Terabyte Dr.
Las Vegas, NV 89102

June 17, 2015

Deborah Harper
Simmons & Simmons
983 Blue Chip Dr.
Las Vegas, NV 89105

Dear Deborah:

I hope you are having a good week. My friend Jeremy Stone who works there sent me your way. I know you've been travelling frequently over the last few months, but I just wanted to let you know I am still very interested in the part-time Assistant Art Director position if it is still open.

Creative project management and attentive customer service have been crucial to my success in my most recent positions. Further, my experience with direct mail (Zing Printing) and email campaigns (Pinkleton Productions) as well as creating graphic, web, and written content would also be an asset in such a position with Simmons & Simmons.

When you have a moment, please give me a call. I would love to meet—even if briefly—to discuss your needs, see how my skills are a fit, and answer any questions you may have. My résumé is enclosed if you need another copy. Thank you for your time and consideration.

Sincerely,

Lara Pinkleton
(999) 555-1212
lpinkleton.com/portfolio.html

JOB SEARCH LOG

STATUS	COMPANY	PHONE	NAME & TITLE	RECEPTIONIST	POSITION OPEN	NOTES/ADDRESS	SOURCE (& POSTE	EMAIL	URL OF JOB POSTING
3/22 fc 3/20 fc'd–she's ooo	Horseshoe Marketing & Adve	(615) 123-0001	Cameron Evans, Pr	Lila	Jr. Account Executive	downtown St. Louis	per Angela Pigglesw	cameron@ho	www.horseshoemktg.com/jobs/aE7g4
6/15 fu, 4/16 says "We will ke	Mandy's Foods	(615) 123-0002	Steven Swanson	Pat	Merchandiser	should be 105 Memorial Dr. St. L	Indeed 3/18	not listed	http://careers.mandysfoods.com/us/m
3/19 em'd to apply via CL	Say What Promotions	(615) 123-0003	not listed		Promotional Marketing S	430 Lynch St. - Unit E, St. Louis,	Craigslist 3/18	dlpr9-437351	http://stl.craigslist.org/mar/437351685
6/6 fe'd Al to see if new perso	Best of Show Equipment Co	(615) 123-0004	Al Acane, GM	n/a	Graphic Designer	513 North 12th St., St. Louis, MO	Their website	al@bosrec.co	www.bosrec.com/careers

LETTER OF HIRE REQUEST/SUMMARY EMAIL

Dear Mr. Walker:

Thank you for the opportunity to interview yesterday and the subsequent job offer today for the Accounting Supervisor position. I can assure you that you will be pleased with my performance for your branch office. So we are both on the same page with the results of our last meeting, respectfully I would like to ask that you would email or fax a signed offer letter on your letterhead including the things below as I understand them.

Job title -
Salary (or pay structure) -
Benefits - ((401k, relocation allowance, signing bonus, when insurance coverage begins, etc.))
Vacation time -
Work days and hours -
Office/work space -

Understanding that ___ ((Here, note any trips, volunteer work, or special appointments you have on your calendar that conflict with work and anything else you feel strongly about or that should be documented in writing.))

After the receipt of your letter and my giving notice to my current employer, I will let you know the soonest I can begin with ABC Company. Thank you for your time. I look forward to being a part of ABC very soon.

Sincerely,

Bert Wigglesworth

NETWORKING EVENTS

1. **BNI: Hillsboro Rd. Chapter** - meets every Thur. at 7am at the Hampton Inn just North of Green Hills Mall. There is a $5 fee, and it includes breakfast. The meeting lasts approximately 90 minutes. Formal and very structured but a laid-back group. Membership strongly encouraged. Each attendee gets 30 seconds to share what their business is about each time, so you will know what everyone does even if you don't have the chance to meet as you network. More info at: http://bnitennessee.com.

2. **Entrepreneur Center** - monthly Tue. happy hour mixer and end of the month coffee. First, register for the prerequisite orientation at http://www.ec.co/entrepreneurship-orientation-1. More info at: http://www.ec.co/events

3. **Nashville Chamber of Commerce**: East - 1st Wed., 8:15am, location varies; no rsvp. More info at:
    http://web.nashvillechamber.com/cwt/external/wcpages/wcevents/eventsstartpage.aspx?o e=true

4. **American Marketing Association, Nashville** - usually 2nd Tue., 5-7pm, rsvp at http://nashvilleama.org

5. **Nashcocktail** - 3rd Tue. at Sam's Bar, 6-8pm, rsvp at nashcocktail.com

6. **Connect Nashville** - 3rd Tue., location varies, 5-7pm, join/rsvp www.meetup.com/connectnashville

NETWORKING LOG & TARGET COMPANIES LIST

NETWORKING LIST

STATUS	1st NAME	LAST NAME	COMPANY	PHONE	EMAIL	TITLE	ADDRESS	CITY	ST	ZIP	WEBSITE	NOTES	PRIOR SOURCE/REFERRED E
DONE - 3/12 called 1 last time--was with	Peachateria	Johnson	Copy Masters	555-790-3340	pjohnson@	Customer S	9401 Malard Ln S	St. Louis	MO	63103	copymasters.com/workforus		Met through Tom Angelis at Tom
3/4 em'd for nm. 2/27 LICR'd	Jimbo	Schmidt	Jslice Design	? - get when he c	jschmidt@de	Owner/Grap	TBA	St. Louis	MO	63104	designnbyj.com		Met his brother at Chamber mixer

TARGET COMPANIES

STATUS	1st NAME	LAST NAME	COMPANY	PHONE	EMAIL	TITLE	ADDRESS	CITY	ST	ZIP	WEBSITE	NOTES	PRIOR SOURCE/REFERRED E	
5/30 reqd nm. 5/22 LICR'd=accptd 6/12	Emilie	Guarini	The Design House	555-514-7510	eg@dh.co	Senior Acc	903 10th Ave S. #	St. Louis	MO	63101	thedh.com/jobs	Has been very nice at	Reference USA	a
6/20 we'll meet. 6/18 spoke. 6/17 lvm. 6/	Claire	Zender	Bookster	555-292-8921	czender@	Marketing N	2143 Belter Ave	St. Louis	MO	63102	bookster.com/careers	A couple of good jobs	Courtney Higgenbottom	b

NETWORKING MEETING INTERVIEW QUESTIONS

Ricardo Montero	**Tango Press** - 617 Murfreesboro Pike Phoenix, AZ
999-7118	rmontero@tpress.com
	Owner
Meeting:	7/7/15 - 3:30

How know Jennifer Chester? (mutual colleague)

Are you from TX originally?

In what part of town do you live?

What did you do before Tango Press?

(A few specific questions about the company):
How long has Tango been around?

Do you run more offset than digital printing?

Do you accept any B to C or just B to B/larger jobs?

Do Tango's customers tend to be more from 1 type industry?

Do you attend many networking events?

Have you ever tried ___ (the association you're a member of or thinking about joining)

(Give Elevator Speech)

Can you think of anyone I should network with?

Are there any companies I should look into?

NETWORKING MEETING REQUEST EMAIL EXAMPLES

Hi Lindsay:
I hope you are having a good week. When Ken Williams and I talked last, he suggested connecting with someone at Acme Widgets.

I am networking in efforts toward an electrical engineering job in the Denver area, writing a book, and working on a couple of other projects. Would you have a day next week we could meet for 10 or 15 minutes? I would love to get your advice and input as well as see how I could help you.

Your Name
linkedin.com/in/yourlinkedinurl

Hi Nate:
I hope you are having a good week. Thank you for connecting at LinkedIn. I am networking in efforts toward an electrical engineering job in the Denver area, writing a book, and working on a couple of other projects. Would you have a day next week we could meet for 10 or 15 minutes? I would love to get your advice and input as well as see how I could help you.

Your Name
linkedin.com/in/yourlinkedinurl

Hi Lynn:
Hope your week is off to a good start. I don't believe we have had the chance to meet at any of the ___ (association) events. (I joined in June, and it has been such a great experience.) I was talking to Millie Bowers at last night's mixer. She suggested connecting with you. I am working on some new career opportunities and starting to look at different companies in the Austin area. I would love to get your advice and input as well as learn more about your business. Would you have a day next week we could meet for 10-15 minutes or so?

Your Name
linkedin.com/in/yourlinkedinurl

Hi Doug:
Because of my work with the Memphis chapter of the XYZ Association, I occasionally talk to colleagues who need a web site. Also, I am working on some new career opportunities and starting to look at different companies in the Jackson area. I would love to get your advice and input as well as learn more about the current state of website design. Would you have a day this week we could meet for 10-15 minutes or so?

Your Name
linkedin.com/in/yourlinkedinurl

NETWORKING THANK-YOU NOTES

Hi Ken,
Thank you again for your time yesterday. It was good getting to know you and more about ABC Company. I appreciate your keeping me in mind if you hear of a position that's a good fit for me. And I'll keep you in mind as I network if I hear of anyone in need of what ABC Company can do.

Hi John,
Thank you again for your time yesterday. It was good getting to know you and more about what's going on at Avazo University now days. Thanks for the contacts, ideas, and keeping an ear out if you hear of a position that's a good fit for me. Have a good weekend and hope to see you at an AMA (association) event soon.

Hi Paul,
Thank you again for your time Thursday. It was good meeting you and learning more about Zither Printing. I appreciate the leads (I stopped by Rogers Design yesterday) and your keeping me in mind if you hear of a position that's a good fit for me or if you have any overflow design work. Let me know if I can assist you in any way. Have a good week.

OLDER JOBS AND ADDITIONAL INFO

Name of Company
Address:
Phone:
VOE (verification of employment) Phone:
My Supervisor:
My Title:
Dates of Employment:
Pay – starting/ending:
Duties:
Company Awards:
Major Accomplishments, including numerical facts/statistics:
Example:
556 jobs quoted
393 jobs coordinated
71% conversion rate from quoted to orders placed

Name of Company
Address:
Phone:
VOE (verification of employment) Phone:
My Supervisor:
My Title:
Dates of Employment:
Pay – starting/ending:
Duties:
Company Awards:
Major Accomplishments, including numerical facts/statistics:

Name of Company
Address:
Phone:
VOE (verification of employment) Phone:
My Supervisor:
My Title:
Dates of Employment:
Pay – starting/ending:
Duties:
Company Awards:
Major Accomplishments, including numerical facts/statistics:

RECRUITER FIRST CONTACT EMAIL

Dear Chad:
It was good talking this morning. Just to recap, I'm currently looking for:
  • A permanent full-time position
  • In marketing, graphic design, or project management
  • In the greater San Bernadino area
  • $45,000 minimum

I would be happy to come in and meet with you if you would like. Just let me know if you need anything else and what the next step is. Have a good week.

Jerry Varnedeau
(999) 555-1212
www.jerryvarnedeau.com/portfolio.html

SARs (SITUATION-ACTION-RESULT)

• A time when I had to go above and beyond the call of duty in order to get a job done.

• A time when I had too many things to do and I had to prioritize my tasks.

• What is my typical way of dealing with conflict? Give an example.

• A time when I used my fact-finding skills to solve a problem. / An example of when I had to take steps to study a problem and make a decision.

• A time when I anticipated a potential problem and developed preventive measures.

• The most complex assignment I ever had and my role?

• Examples of job experiences that were satisfying. Dissatisfying?

• For what kind of supervisor do I work best? (Characteristics and example)

• A time when I had too many things to do and I had to prioritize my tasks.

What are my weaknesses?

STRENGTHS/QUESTIONS/TELL ME ABOUT YOURSELF

- **Autonomy**
- **Attention to detail and organizational skills**
- **Fast learner**
- **Follow up and communication skills**
- **High productivity**

My Goals:
Be settled into an industry
Doing something I enjoy
Using my talents and skills to the benefit of the company
Being fairly compensated

Tell Me About Yourself: (up to 2 minutes)
I grew up in Kansas and did my undergrad and grad work there. I visited Los Angeles a few times and loved it, moving here in 2001 to work in the music business. I served as the key person at 2 record labels as far as driving staff and vendors to coordinate everything so that over 100 projects released by deadline in under 2 years. Most recently, I worked in a creative-project management role with Cool Stuff Printing until they did some financial restructuring and staff reduction. Currently, I'm seeking a new opportunity in which I can continue to exercise my passion for creativity and design along with more left-brained strengths such as project management and communications.

Second/Final Interview Questions:
- Salary/Pay rate?
- Hours are a bit flexible?
- Vacation policy?
- Frequency of evaluations/raises?
- Chance for promotion/advancement: what do you see as the growth path for advancement from this position?
- Will I have an office?
- Is there a relocation allowance?
- How is employee performance evaluated as far as efforts toward raises and advancement?
- What would you like to see accomplished in the first 3 months after hire?

NOTE: If you have limitations or shortcomings in your skills or knowledge, be up-front with the interviewer about this in the second interview stage. You can button it up by emphasizing that you are happy to do trainings in off hours to get up to speed.

T-STYLE COVER LETTER *(page 1 of 2)*

Lara Pinkleton
11 Terabyte Dr.
Las Vegas, NV 89102

May 13, 2015

Deborah Harper
Simmons & Simmons
983 Blue Chip Dr.
Las Vegas, NV 89105

Dear Deborah:

This morning I was pleased to see your posting at careerbuilder.com for the **Marketing Manager** position you are seeking to fill because it appears to be a strong match with my experience and interests. For your reference, I have included several key points from the job description vs. my background.

Requirements/Duties	My Qualifications
Must have excellent communication skills, both written and verbal. Review, edit, and rewrite marketing copy to appropriately describe products and ensure proper grammar.	Created, wrote, and designed monthly newsletter serviced to all branch employees and clients (Zing Marketing Group). Wrote bios, press releases, ad copy, etc. to brand, market, and promote music acts in the greater Las Vegas area. Freelance album reviewer for about.com (Marketing Director - Pinkleton Productions, 2001-present).
Assist with local market planning and analysis. Assist with creation of scorecards and campaign management reporting.	14+ years branding/marketing, consulting, planning, designing, and website authoring for freelance clients to achieve the objectives of their marketing strategies (Pinkleton Productions).
Media relations via email and social media. Active social media participant.	Implemented and managed social media marketing campaigns for clients (including writing, content creation and deployment) in order to optimize client search engine rankings (Pinkleton Productions). Regularly using Facebook, LinkedIn, Wordpress/blogging, email, etc. for personal interaction as well as professional networking and promotion.

T-STYLE COVER LETTER *(page 2 of 2)*

My résumé is attached. I am very interested in this position and look forward to hearing back from you about the next step. Thank you for your time and consideration.

Sincerely,

Lara Pinkleton

NOTES:

www.ingramcontent.com/pod-product-compliance
Lightning Source LLC
Chambersburg PA
CBHW051336200326

41519CB00026B/7445